# Performance Culture

## Drive Profits & Create a Great Workplace

Written by:

Dallas Romanowski

Copyright © 2016 Dallas Romanowski

All rights reserved.

ISBN-13: 978-1478295921

# THE PERFORMANCE CULTURE STORY

We believe:
- People deserve a chance to be great and work in an environment they love;
- That an organization's culture should build a sense of community while fulfilling its mission; and that
- Managers should be more than supervisors, they should also coach and mentor their employees.

Company culture drives an organization's competitive advantage because it determines how things are done and how people behave -- an advantage that is difficult to copy. When your culture drives performance and fosters team chemistry, it's known as a Performance Culture. While each organization's culture is unique, a Performance Culture includes a pattern of remarkably consistent behaviors known as core values. We believe leaders who focus on people will produce the returns required for an organization to be successful.

We developed the Performance Culture System™ (PCS) to ensure behaviors are never ignored while pursuing business results. Great performing organizations require great coaches. The Performance Culture platform provides leaders and supervisors with an agile, effective system to guide the process and capture the information needed to support performance improvement efforts. Performance Culture provides employees a process to achieve their personal and career goals through coaching, feedback, and clear expectations.

Mediocrity should not be accepted and organizations should not be weighed down by disengaged employees simply because leaders don't have the courage or energy to hold team members accountable. The Performance Culture platform enables managers to have crucial conversations that help team members maximize their potential.

The Performance Culture System™ was developed by Cornerstone Business Advisors based on the work it has done with 100+ clients, many of whom are qualified for INC's 5000 List of Fastest Growing Companies. Cornerstone, founded in 2007, realized there was a pattern of success while working with companies that defied the odds during the Great Recession (2008 – 2011). This pattern included four simple elements: People, Process, Strategy and Leadership. Dallas Romanowski, the founder of Cornerstone, originally published the Performance Culture book in August 2012 to help leaders implement the four elements of a Performance Culture. This book serves as a coaching guide for leaders who are ready to implement the Performance Culture System.

Initially the tools used to implement the Performance Culture System included multiple templates (spreadsheets, presentations and forms). While these templates were effective, it became cumbersome to manage and did not produce the reporting leadership teams needed to track organizational performance. In 2013, our team set out to find a web-based system to model our coaching process but could not find one that met these requirements:

1. Performance & Talent Management functionality must be able to produce the Performance Values Matrix – A simple 2 x 2 grid that evaluates both performance and workplace behaviors.

2. The Business Planning Templates must be easy to use – Most leadership teams fail to maintain management systems that become too administrative to manage. It has to be easy!

3. The system has to be cost effective – Most systems evaluated with the required user functionality cost between $70 to $300 per user per year. This price point is way too high.

Since we could not find a system that met these requirements, we decided to build our own and began using it with clients in 2013. The initial clients provided very valuable feedback. This feedback helped Cornerstone develop a viable product that could significantly scale and is now available as a web-based application (PerformanceCulture.com).

In late 2014, the Cornerstone team decided to spin off the Performance Culture System into a new software and training company.

## Results from the Performance Culture System

One of the most revealing findings our team has found with the Performance Culture System is the impact the Performance Values Matrix has on employees and leaders. The visual representation of how an employee is performing does more than any number or comment can do. All employees want to be Stars and when they see themselves in the Star category, it provides tremendous satisfaction.

We have also seen rapid improvement by employees in the matrix's other three categories. Managers use the Performance Values Matrix as a framework to coach employees. Engaged employees quickly adopt coaching feedback while disengaged employees will often self select out of the organization.

Employees enjoy using the Performance Culture System, something you rarely hear about with other performance management software. The business results have been amazing. There are numerous testimonies about how the Performance

Culture process has helped increased revenue and profit. Many business owners also say they have more time to work on the business versus in it because they have elevated their team and delegated responsibilities.

More than a hundred companies have implemented the system. 100% of these clients have said the system has more than met their expectations. Our success is not only based on the system functionality and ease of use, but also the training we provide.

# DEDICATION

There are so many people I would like to thank. This book would not be possible without the time others invested in mentoring me.

Melissa Phillippi, Co-Founder of Performance Culture, – I'm proud to be your partner! Launching our company would not have happened without your leadership and personal commitment.

The original Performance Culture Team (Melissa, Amy, Jen & Mike) -- You guys rock! Plus all the Cornerstone Partners who have advised us along the way.

Our original Investors (Rich & Brian) – Thank you for believing in us and your coaching!

Cornerstone Clients — Thank you for giving our firm and myself the opportunity to serve.

Cornerstone Partners — Thank you for investing your time and energy into our firm and what you do for our clients.

Gretchen Romanowski — Thank you for your editing and advice in publishing this book.

Dad — Thank you for always believing in me and your support over the years.

Mom — Thank you for giving me the entrepreneurial spirit.

My wife and three children — Thank you for all you do and putting up with my long hours; you are the core focus of my life.

# CONTENTS

| | | |
|---|---|---|
| 1 | Introduction | 1 |
| 2 | Performance Culture Overview | 7 |
| 3 | Leadership Effectiveness | 17 |
| 4 | Niche Strategy | 29 |
| 5 | People Management | 39 |
| 6 | Process Excellence | 55 |
| 7 | Succession Planning & Exit Strategies | 65 |
| 8 | Conclusion & Next Steps | 71 |
| 9 | Coach's Toolbox (Templates & Implementer Guide) | 75 |
| | 9.1 Personal Vision | 76 |
| | 9.2 Company Vision & Mission | 78 |
| | 9.3 Company Foundation | 79 |
| |     A. Accountability Chart | |
| |     B. Employee Evaluation | |
| |     C. Performance Values Team Matrix | |
| |     D. Value Chain | |
| |     E. Scorecard | |
| |     F. Current State Assessment | |
| | 9.4 Leadership Assessment | 85 |
| | 9.5 Niche Strategy / Competitive Advantage | 96 |
| | 9.6 Process Excellence | 98 |
| | 9.7 90-Day Plan | 101 |
| | 9.8 Weekly Team Meeting Agenda | 106 |
| | 9.9 Coaching Engagement Project Plan | 107 |

# CHAPTER 1
# INTRODUCTION

*PERFORMANCE CULTURE* provides a simplified approach to create a company culture that increases business value, profitability and workplace satisfaction — an approach that has proven to work in the companies we coach. Many of our clients have significantly grown their business by implementing the four elements of Performance Culture. These elements include Effective Leadership, Niche Strategy, People Management and Process Excellence.

The idea to write this book occurred while I was recapping the success of many of our clients during the height of the recession that began in 2008. While many companies were struggling, many of our clients were growing. In some cases the growth was amazing – 25% to 200% APR. We created a list of our fastest growing clients and looked for commonalities among the successful companies. What we found was revealing.

While the successful companies were doing many things differently, we did find four common traits. These traits included effective leadership, niche strategies, a great team & workplace (people) and process excellence. The company owners led in a way that earned the will of their team. They hired right, communicated expectations and held team members accountable for results. The companies focused on very specific target markets and offered unique products and services. Their niche strategies enabled them to win more clients and earn higher profit margins. The leaders focused on process excellence and made sure processes were documented, followed and constantly improved.

Performance Culture helps you develop strong leaders, high performing employees and a great company culture. It will create habits that drive profitability and increase your company value. The Brax Story is a perfect example of this.

## The Brax Story

Brax, Ltd., is not much different than most small businesses. It has less than 50 employees, and is still owned by the two founders, Pete Hexter and John Alexander. Brax is a manufacturer of licensed and promotional products and offers a unique fulfillment service that helps non-profits fundraise. While Brax has been very successful, it has experienced challenges common to businesses that are either growing rapidly or facing challenges in the marketplace. In this case, Brax's challenges were based on outgrowing management practices — practices that used to work when there were just a handful of employees.

In the beginning, the owners worked hard to create an employee-friendly, family-business atmosphere. The overall company structure was fairly loose and most new hires were family members, friends or friends of friends. This worked well for Brax in the beginning when it was a very small business filled with entrepreneurial, start-up passion. The owners were able to keep their eyes and ears close to the ground, handle issues as they arose and react quickly.

However, as Brax grew it became more and more difficult to keep on top of everything. The business was becoming more complex because of more customers, more employees, more suppliers and higher working-capital requirements. Daily fire drills became the norm — especially during their busy season. The owners could not free themselves from day-to-day operations without worrying.

Achieving the owners' personal visions of spending more time on strategic activities and less time at work looked bleak. The owners also began to question the sustainability of their business growth without delegating management responsibilities, increasing employee productivity and improving overall workplace morale. While the business was not in jeopardy and customer satisfaction was high, **change had to happen** to sustain revenue growth and free the owners from day-to-day operational responsibilities.

Both Pete and John were committed to change and felt the Performance Culture System had potential. Brax engaged our firm to guide them through the implementation process. We began by assessing the company's strengths and weaknesses using 360-degree leadership interviews. Our findings validated the owners' concerns. Employee morale was down and there was mistrust among the team. Employees felt micro-managed and there was a lack of communication. The company's mission was not shared by all and office politics were high.

However, the interviews did provide good news. The focus on customer satisfaction was throughout and the employees believed the owners genuinely cared about them. The confidential 360-degree interviews also increased the trust and rapport I had with the team as their Business Coach. This trust increased the team's willingness to adopt the management practices we would later implement as part of the Performance Culture System.

Fortunately Brax had already created a winning niche strategy — one of the four elements of Performance Culture. So our implementation plan focused on the remaining three: Leadership Effectiveness, People Management and Process Excellence. The leadership team integrated these elements in the company culture over a four-month period.

The engagement significantly improved the Brax culture and created a foundation to support future growth. Brax revisited their company vision and mission and made sure it was shared by all. This has given the team a common purpose and a framework to identify Critical Success Factors (CSF). Overall focus and time management also improved by prioritizing company initiatives every quarter.

Process documentation and training has made operations more consistent and turn around times have decreased. The Sales Team has a playbook to follow and is frequently coached on how to increase sales and delight customers using the "Brax Way". There are fewer errors because guidelines for customer orders and fulfillment are followed. The financial processes have identified key metrics to gauge company performance and are measured daily. During team meetings, managers are always looking for ways to improve processes. This has increased overall efficiency and profitability.

Accountability has increased with written action plans, 90-day planning sessions and weekly leadership team meetings. Maverick employees and low performers self-select out of the company and high performers are rewarded and recognized. Office politics have decreased by simply removing titles and creating an accountability chart. Employees have clear expectations in terms of both performance and behaviors. Trust and morale have improved because of candid, frequent communication.

Pete and John worry less about the company and focus more time on strategic initiatives. They also spend less time in the business since they have a key leader who is managing day-to-day operations. The Performance Culture System has improved the leadership abilities of the entire management team. When the timing is right, the owners can now implement a Leadership Succession Plan that will maximize their business' value and provide attractive retirement options.

The Brax Story should give you confidence the Performance Culture System works. You simply need to trust the process and stay committed.

## About Brax

Brax, Ltd., is headquartered in Wilmington, N.C., and manufactures licensed promotional products in multiple geographies. It is most known for Spirit Cups – cups that have a collegiate or professional sports team logo imprinted with 3-D technology. The company provides non-profit organizations a unique way to achieve their fundraising objectives. Youth sports teams raise funds by selling promotional items manufactured by Brax. The products sell extremely well and Brax manages most of the fulfillment process—which requires less work from the volunteers. As a result of a solid niche strategy and a unique value proposition, Brax has grown exponentially over the past seven years and has helped hundreds of non-profit organizations achieve their fundraising goals.

PERFORMANCE CULTURE

# CHAPTER 2
# PERFORMANCE CULTURE OVERVIEW

The Performance Culture System will help you develop the right habits to grow your business to new levels of success. This may mean changing the habits that were initially required to make your company successful and it may mean some hard choices, but the reward is worth the effort.

In most cases, when entrepreneurs first launch their business they have to do everything. Not because they want to, but because they HAVE to. There is simply not enough cash flow to hire all the people you need. If you were not a control freak to start with, you eventually became one. There was no other choice — your livelihood depended on the success of your company — and control turned into habit, and we all know that some habits can be bad.

Habits are natural phenomena of human behavior. We develop habits because we learn certain behaviors produce rewards. If we like the instant gratification of the reward, we repeat the behavior, even if the repeated behavior will not produce a long-term positive outcome. Why else would people smoke, use drugs or drink excessively? Or run their business in a reactionary, short-sighted way?

Developing a Performance Culture that produces long-term benefit takes discipline and commitment — the essential elements required to create good habits. However, before you implement the Performance Culture System, it's important to recognize the bad habits your company may have as well as understand how you can develop good habits.

Examples of Bad Behaviors (Habits)

- Micro-management/Lack of Delegation — Business owners and/or leaders that are overly involved in too many aspects of the business because they are worried about failure

- Constant Fire Drills — Managers focused on solving immediate challenges versus strategic planning and continuous process improvement

- Immediate Gratification — Employees focused on immediate personal benefit versus mid to long term strategic results (i.e., What's in it for me today); Owners who spend all the profits versus investing in future growth

- Directing versus Motivating — Leading by force versus developing employees to be their best

- Silo Mentality/Mavericks — Focusing on individual effort versus the team's performance; Lack of trust inside the organization; office politics, et cetera

- Lack of Accountability — Allowing employees to get away with bad performance — "It's too much work to coach the employee, he'll do better next time" but he never does

- Hiring Too Quickly and Firing Too Slowly — Putting off hiring until it's absolutely needed and ending up with a subpar employee or not firing soon enough and being stuck with an undesirable employee or behavior

- Lack of Communication — Leaders who view meetings as a waste of time (Note: Meetings can be a waste of time if not facilitated correctly, but if the meetings are managed correctly, meetings build team rapport and ensure alignment with company priorities)

- Opportunism — Chasing everything versus focusing on what you can do best; Pursuing "strategies of the month" versus management discipline

If you can relate to one or more of these negative behaviors or have noticed unhealthy habits inside your company, you are not alone. Performance Culture will help you change these behaviors and develop positive habits that will increase profit and lead to long-term sustainability.

In the book, <u>The Power of Habit: Why We Do What We Do in Life and Business</u> author Charles Duhigg explains how business leaders achieved success by focusing on the patterns that shape every aspect of our lives. The Performance Culture System will show you a set of patterns to achieve success for you and your company. These patterns include:

- **Effective Leadership** — Three rules to become a great leader

- **Niche Strategy** — Tips on how to create a compelling value proposition and competitive advantage

- **People Management** — Simple Human Resource Management methods to hire right and motivate employees to do their best

- **Process Excellence** — A simplified framework to create a scalable operation that delivers consistency and quality

## Hitting the Ceiling

"Hitting the ceiling" — is a phenomenon that occurs in almost every business at some point and is usually caused by one or two things: (1) Increased management complexity driven by more employees, customers and/or partners; (2) Changes in Industry (market size, increased competition, disruptive technologies, government regulation and customer buying preferences).

When companies hit the ceiling, we often refer to this as an evolutionary period. How companies manage this transition will have a direct impact on future growth and sustainability. There are three potential outcomes for companies going through this transition:

1. *Leadership implements the right changes* (organizational structure, operational processes, business strategy and marketing/sales plan), and positions the company for growth and increased profitability.

2. *Leadership lacks the vision to grow or doesn't recognize the need to change* — Profit margins tend to erode and mid to long-term sustainability is at risk.

3. *Leadership recognizes the need to change, but fails to make the right changes* — Wrong decisions cause the once successful company to fail.

> **Cornerstone's coaching approach is designed to not only help business leaders guide their company through evolutionary periods, but also provide a simplified approach to implement positive change and hold teams accountable for results.**

# "Hitting the Ceiling"

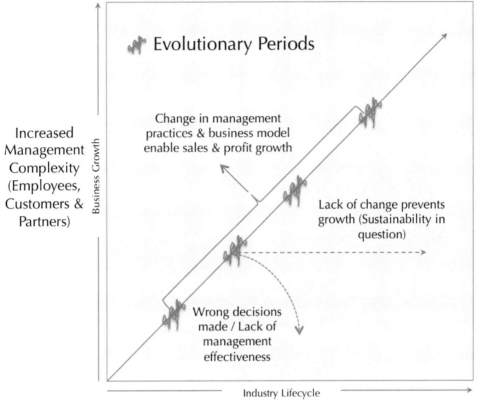

## Position Your Company for Success with the Four Elements

The first element, **Effective Leadership**, is the cornerstone for transforming your company culture into a performance culture. Without effective leadership, the remaining three elements are meaningless. Conversely, effective leaders will transcend their peers and find it much easier to implement the principles in this book.

The second element, **Niche Strategy**, is the foundation for building or increasing your competitive advantage. It includes your Unique Value Proposition (UVP) — your way of standing out from the competition. With a solid business strategy, it will be easier to increase profits and your business value.

The third element, **People Management**, simplifies the complexity of managing a growing enterprise and helps you develop a performance culture. It provides a method to determine the right seats and match those seats with the right people. The planning section of People Management enables you to focus on your *Critical Success Factors* (CSF) and provides a means for open, candid communication within your team.

The fourth element, **Process Excellence**, creates a system and scorecard that enables your company to grow. It documents your value chain — your way of acquiring customers and delivering value. A well-defined value chain increases your ability to scale your organization. Process not only ensures quality and efficiency, but also provides a framework for continuous improvement.

Implementing these four elements in your business is a process itself and requires discipline and commitment. Initially, this may mean working harder in the short term, but your work/life balance will improve and you will have higher profitability. After implementing this process, you should see significant positive change within three to six months (if not sooner).

Avoiding Past Failures

Business owners are always interested in improving their business. Often business owners try "strategies of the month" to increase profitability. These management practices are frequently ineffective because either the strategy was not well thought-out or the leaders did not have the discipline to carry through and hold team members accountable. The Four Elements will work for your company if you avoid these mistakes and are committed to staying the course.

## The Performance Culture Coaching Process™

The Performance Culture Coaching Process begins by first understanding your personal vision. Your personal vision[1] should define your personal goals and provide an outline of what you personally want. We start with your personal vision because it will impact the direction you take your company.

After defining your personal vision, we evaluate the *leadership effectiveness* of yourself and key leaders. During this step, we validate what's working well and identify areas for improvement. As part of this process, you will define your company's vision and mission and share it with all.

With your company vision and mission in place, we evaluate your *niche strategy*. If you already have a niche strategy and solid competitive advantage, we quickly move onto the next step. If you don't, we help you identify ways to create a competitive advantage in the market place. Smaller companies have an advantage over larger competitors because it is easier for smaller companies to carve out niche value propositions focused on very specific target markets.

The next step, *people management*, begins by defining the right seats and evaluating your current team members. This evaluation not only measures performance, but also behaviors. Once you are satisfied you have the right seats and right people identified, we create a 90-Day Plan. The 90-Day Plan includes Critical Success Factors[2] (CSFs) and action plans to achieve your CSFs. To achieve traction, we provide a structure for weekly leadership meetings. This structure ensures the meeting time is productive and wisely used.

The last step is *process excellence*, the essential element to build a scalable organization that can continue to grow without day-to-day operational involvement from the owner(s). Process will improve quality, decrease operating costs and

---

[1] The Alternative Board's® (TAB) Strategic Business Leadership® (SBL) Program begins by first

[2] SBL is an issued based strategic planning methodology developed by TAB and includes Critical Success Factors

provide Key Performance Indicators (KPIs) to gauge company health. Once implemented, you will find it much easier to focus on strategic initiatives to grow your business.

**THE PERFORMANCE CULTURE COACHING PROCESS**

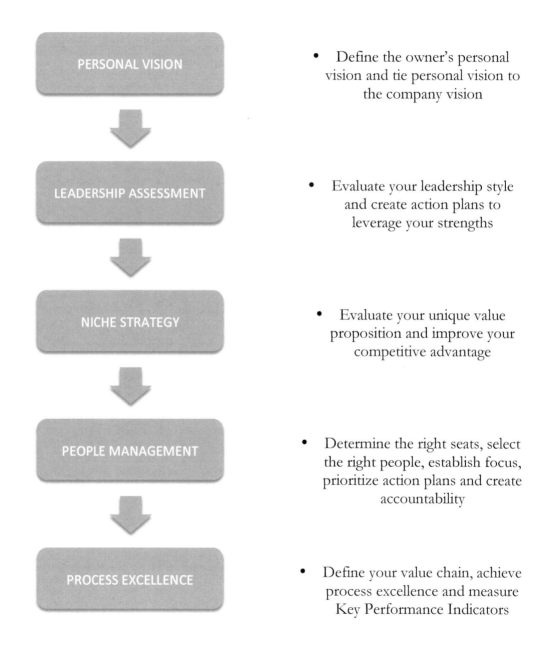

Nine Lessons Learned from *THE POWER OF HABIT*

1. Habits are formed when a cue motivates an individual to act in a certain way because he/she associates a reward with the cue and behavior (Cue > Behavior > Reward).

2. Effective change can begin by creating just one good habit. This habit will motivate the organization to develop additional good habits. Start with one keystone habit that can create enormous positive energy inside your organization.

3. The best performing companies are those that have routines.

4. The worst performing companies do not have routines; the leaders do not recognize the importance of process.

5. Avoid constant fire drills. Constant stress erodes a person's will power. Proper work/life balance will increase a person's ability to perform at work and make better decisions.

6. The best way to increase will power is to build positive habits.

7. Positive habits increase self-discipline. Research shows self-discipline is a better predicator of success than a high IQ.

8. Company habits improve a leader's ability to delegate. Employees displaying habits feel more in control of their work and decisions, a key workplace motivator.

9. Five tenants to support positive habits and the Performance Culture System:

    1. Create a company vision and mission shared by all. Help employees understand how their personal vision will be achieved by achieving the company vision.

    2. Ensure consistency through effective leadership and process.

3. Reward and recognize good behaviors.

4. Hold employees accountable. Enforce consequences for negative behaviors; when an employee violates the company culture, he/she must go.

5. A written plan with weekly updates will encourage good habits to flourish. Research has shown that people on diets or on exercise plans do better when they write down their plan and document their activities in a journal. The same is true for the Performance Culture System. Writing down your plans creates clarity and forces you to think through actions.

# CHAPTER 3
# EFFECTIVE LEADERSHIP

A leader leads by example, not by force, and must earn the will of his or her team, as a person's will cannot be mandated. If you have your people's will, they will support you through your toughest challenges. Your employees should believe that you place your priorities on the organization before yourself. In many ways, this is servant leadership. Strong leaders recognize the contributions of the team before his or her efforts as a leader. In the book, *Think Big, Act Small*, one of the predominant findings is that most successful privately held companies are led by very modest leaders.

As a company leader, you should evaluate your entire leadership team (including yourself) using these three principles:

- Has the leader earned the will of their team?
- Does the leader communicate clearly and wisely?
- Does the leader hold team members accountable for their actions?

## Earn the Will of your Team

Tom Morris, a philosopher and mentor of mine, best described the approach to earn the will of your team through his book, *True Success: The Art of Achievement and the 7 C's of Success*. The 7 C's are:

1. A clear CONCEPTION of what we want, a vivid vision, a goal clearly imagined.

2. A strong CONFIDENCE that we can attain the goal.

3. A focused CONCENTRATION on what it takes to reach the goal.

4. A stubborn CONSISTENCY in pursuing our vision.

5. An emotional COMMITMENT to the importance of what we are doing.

6. A good CHARACTER to guide us and keep us on a proper course.

7. A CAPACITY TO ENJOY the process along the way.

*A clear CONCEPTION of what we want, a vivid vision, a goal clearly imagined.*

Establishing a vision not only prevents you from settling, but also provides a framework to recognize what is important and what is not. A vision will inspire you as well as others. However, before you can create your vision, you must first know yourself. What is really important to you? What are you passionate about? What motivates you?

Knowing who you really are is one of the most difficult things to do – you must dig deep to discover yourself. It involves assessing your strengths and weaknesses as well as what inspires you. Are you willing to settle and just be in the background or do you want to make a difference and bring positive change?

Instead of being a background player, you should know what you want to be. With a clear vision and goal, it is easier to understand what is relevant in your life. For example, when you want something dearly, you begin to recognize everything related to your desire. Without this desire/vision/goal, you will not easily know what you should pay attention to.

*A strong CONFIDENCE that we can attain the goal.*

You are not going to be great if you don't take risks to improve. In some cases, these risks may cause things to worsen temporarily, but these sacrifices will ultimately lead to bigger and better things. You must have confidence that you can overcome the temporary downfalls associated with risk taking.

Champions run ahead of what the current evidence shows will absolutely work. They have initial confidence that their plan will prevail. When things don't go well, leaders have resilient confidence to not let failures keep them down. If business was about making decisions with a known outcome, very few innovations would ever occur.

*A focused CONCENTRATION on what it takes to reach the goal.*

You cannot be all things to all people. When everything is important, nothing is important. The key to concentration is to avoid being distracted by things that are not critical to your success.

Give yourself time to think – you will make better decisions. It's ok to look out the window to deeply contemplate issues and challenges. Think through the possible unintended consequences of your actions and develop plans to counter them.

With your vision in place, determine the three most critical success factors to achieve your vision. Re-prioritize your work day to spend the most time on these critical success factors. During my coaching sessions, I ask leaders to do this exercise every 90 days. It's amazing how much companies accomplish when leaders and their team understand company priorities and focus their work effort accordingly.

*A stubborn CONSISTENCY in pursuing our vision.*

Do your actions match your words? Do your actions support your goals? Consistency is about tying everything together. Consistency creates trust and increases a person's ability to lead through influence rather than authority.

Inconsistency often leads to Dysfunctional Organizations because it creates ignorance, indifference and negative inertia. To illustrate this point, I've highlighted common feedback from employees during 360-Degree assessments:

- Ignorance – *"I don't know what's really important. Company priorities are always changing and we often have strategies of the month without follow through."*

- Indifference – *"Team members are not held accountable for their work effort and many projects start, but don't end."*
*"At some point, you stop caring about the collective whole and just do what you have to do to keep your job."*
*"My boss talks a big game, but you should see how he acts outside of work."*

- Inertia – *"It will be difficult to change because we have operated this way for such a long time. This IS the culture of our company."*

*An emotional COMMITMENT to the importance of what we are doing.*

People are attracted to people that care. Business is not just about Intellectual Gamesmanship; it's about people working together for a common goal. If we get to know each other on an emotional level, we can do great things together. Most employees will say they have worked hardest for bosses who took time to understand them personally and show appreciation for their effort. People want to feel important and be recognized. Investing time into your employees will increase their loyalty and their receptiveness to constructive feedback. Genuine interest and appreciation of others will always help you win friends and influence people.[3]

> ## Logic versus Emotion
>
> Have you ever tried to make a clear point and influence someone with numbers and tangible proof to no avail? You presented your case and knew that logic would clearly support your position, but by the end of your presentation, you heard, "The numbers make sense, but something just **doesn't feel right**". People's emotions control their decision making much more so than logic.

*A good CHARACTER to guide us and keep us on a proper course.*

Many people can achieve temporary success, but to keep it, you must have strong character. We've all seen people rise quickly and fall quicker, especially at the national level. Just think about politicians, CEOs, actors, religious leaders, and sports figures who dominate the news cycle one week (usually for something they'd rather not be known or remembered for) only to be forgotten the next.

Leaders must have strong character inside and outside of the workplace. I know some folks prefer to have a different life outside of work, but this should not mean a different life with lower standards. The patience and discernment you practice at work should carry over to your personal life, especially with your family.

Leaders will encounter more stressful activities than most. Their capacity to handle stress has enabled them to earn their position as a leader. However, we all have "tipping points" where we take on more than we should handle. Without maintaining a good balance of mind, body and spirit, these tipping points will often lessen one's ability to lead effectively. Pay attention to what your body and subconscious are telling you.

---

[3] *How to Win Friends and Influence People,* Dale Carnegie

*A CAPACITY TO ENJOY the process along the way.*

Life is finite and we only have one shot. There is no "do over". Recognizing this simple truth will help you enjoy the gifts each day brings.

## **Communicate Clearly and Wisely**

While living the 7 C's will earn the will of your team, a leader must still communicate clearly and wisely. This means establishing clear expectations and creating a workplace culture that encourages candor and collaboration. Creating this culture requires a common vision and management discipline – the key focus of the people management chapter in this book.

In addition to management discipline, there is a softer side to effective communication that involves emotional intelligence. We have all heard of the Golden Rule — Treat others the way you want to be treated. While this philosophy does pay dividends, it is not always the best way to approach communication. Adapting your communication style in a way that best resonates with another person will improve your ability to persuade and motivate others.

If you have not taken a behavioral communication assessment, I encourage you to do so. The assessment not only helps you understand your preferred communication style, but also helps you understand where you may need to adapt your style. The assessments typically evaluate four dimensions of behavior:

1. Controlling versus Collaborative
2. Extrovert versus Introvert
3. Tolerance for Change
4. Process versus Creativity

After conducting hundreds of assessments, we have found entrepreneurs' behavioral preferences typically include:

- A need for control

- A desire for continuous change

- A strong preference to solve problems creatively versus following a process

Subjectively, our coaching sessions reveal a similar pattern. Most entrepreneurs we coach launched their business not for money, but because of their desire for control. We've also seen a pattern of behaviors that prefers change and creativity. These behavioral patterns are an asset, but also present challenges when entrepreneurs do not adapt their communication style. The most successful entrepreneurs have learned to adapt their natural style to:

1. Collaborate in a way that improves decision making and sense of buy in.

2. Implement change when needed, but avoid change just for the sake of change.

3. Create systems and processes to support consistency, quality and efficiency (Magic happens when entrepreneurs develop processes and systems to support their creative ideas).

# The four dimensions of behavior as defined by Target Training International

## Dominance  Influence  Steadiness  Compliance

**High** ↑

| Dimension | High | Description | Low |
|---|---|---|---|
| **How you approach & respond to problems and exercise power** | New problems are solved quickly, assertively, and actively. You get to the bottom-line quickly. | | New problems are solved in a controlled, organized way. You think before acting. |
| **How you approach & interact with people** | You meet new people in an outgoing, talkative manner and tend to be gregarious and emotional. | | You meet new people in a quiet, controlled, reserved manner and tend to be emotionally controlled. |
| **How you respond to change, variation and the pace of your environment** | You prefer a controlled, deliberate work environment and value security. | | You prefer a flexible, dynamic, changeable environment and value freedom of expression. |
| **How you respond to procedures and rules set by others and to authority** | You like things done 'the right way,' and believe, "Rules are made to be followed." | | You work independently of the procedures and believe, "Rules are made to be bent or broken." |

**Low** ↓

PERFORMANCE CULTURE

TTI's DISC Leadership Behavioral Profile

> 85% of entrepreneurs we coach are in the highlighted area which is only about 15% of the entire population of people who have completed the TTI Behavioral Assessment. The best entrepreneurial leaders recognize their behavioral style and have learned how to adapt their behaviors to motivate team members.

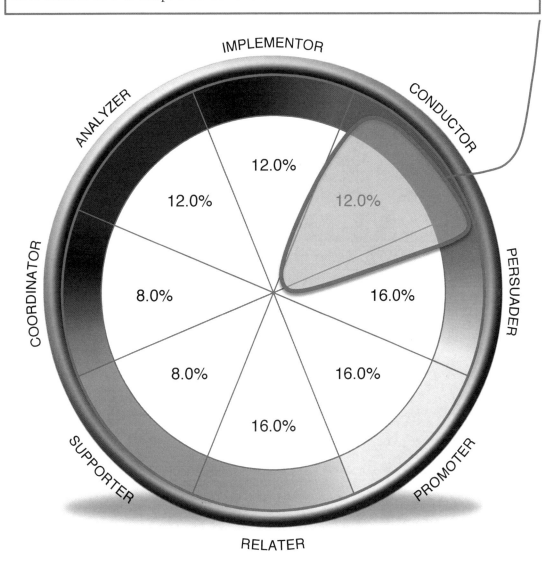

The Leadership Template in the Coach's Toolbox provides communication tips for each behavioral profile.

## Hold Team Members Accountable

Ancient Chinese general and philosopher Sun Tzu stated that if a leader has earned the will of the team and has communicated clearly, then the leader must hold his *direct report* accountable for action. There must be consequences for inaction or under-performing. If you are not willing to enforce a consequence for inaction or under-performance, then you should re-evaluate your expectations or directive. Are your expectations realistic or are you uncomfortable dealing with conflict? If it's the latter, it's a sign of weak leadership.

There will certainly be cases where discretion and judgment will play into the consequences delivered. The key point is to focus your time and energy on your best employees and quickly remove employees that don't fit your culture — it will be better for all in the long run. Holding team members accountable requires as much discipline from the leader as it does from the employees.

Often our coaching engagements include an element of change management to support implementing the Performance Culture System. In many cases there will be at least one employee resisting the change and disrupting the process. Unfortunately this often results in a separation. However, there is a benefit to this consequence because overall buy-in is increased tenfold. In most cases, morale is improved because employees are happy to see the employee with negative behaviors leave.

## Conclusion

In normal environments, it's difficult to distinguish good leaders from great leaders. The difference becomes much more visible in extreme or challenging situations. Leaders who have honed the three leadership principles described in this book will be the ones who can carry your organization through the storms.

These leaders will develop a great workplace environment, a mainstay of your competitive advantage as described in the book *Great by Choice*, by Jim Collins. After researching thousands of companies, Collins and his research team found that the companies that significantly out-performed their peers were the ones who had the best workplace cultures. Employees in these companies rated their workplace environment and job satisfaction higher than their peers.

PERFORMANCE CULTURE

## CHAPTER 4
## NICHE STRATEGY

**"Focusing solely on what you can do better than any other organization is the only path to greatness." Jim Collins, *Good to Great*_**

Niche strategies create competitive advantages for small to medium size businesses. They allow you to differentiate your company from potential competitors by demonstrating an expertise in a particular product or service as well as an in-depth understanding of your clients' unique needs and wants. To illustrate this point, just take a look at INC's Fastest 5,000 growing companies in any year. You will notice the vast majority of these companies are focusing on a unique product, service and/or industry. Our coaching firm has also seen this first hand as many of our clients qualify to be on INC's 5,000 list.

While a niche strategy may make common sense, it is not the most common strategy used among small businesses. If you happen to be one of the few companies that have a solid niche strategy, you can move onto the next chapter -- people management. However, if you're not, this chapter will help you explore ways to refine or develop your competitive advantage.

We start most of our coaching engagements by asking our clients to describe how their company is unique. The most common answers include:

Our company is unique because...

...We provide great customer service

...We deliver a high quality product or service

...We have the best prices

...We win because of our relationships

The challenge is that these answers rarely create competitive advantage and are quite possibly a symptom of eating your own cooking. Your competitors are most likely saying the same thing and feel the same way. I know, you are probably thinking, "But in my case it really is true." Even if it is true, your competitive advantage is not scalable and has a high risk of being diminished.

To create your niche strategy, first answer these three questions:

1. Do we leverage our core strengths and do our strengths provide a competitive advantage? (If we don't have strengths that yield a competitive advantage, how can we develop competitive strengths?)

2. Do we focus on a niche market? (The niche market can be by industry, customer type and / or geography.)

3. What problem/need can my company solve that is not currently being addressed in the market place?

Finding your core strength may be fairly easy. Understanding your competitive differentiation requires a bit of market / competitive research. Too often, I've heard entrepreneurs exclaim how their company is the "only one" when a simple Google search identifies hundreds of competitors. I am not suggesting you focus on your competitors, but to simply understand how to develop a niche strategy that wins.

## THE THREE DIMENSIONS OF A NICHE STRATEGY

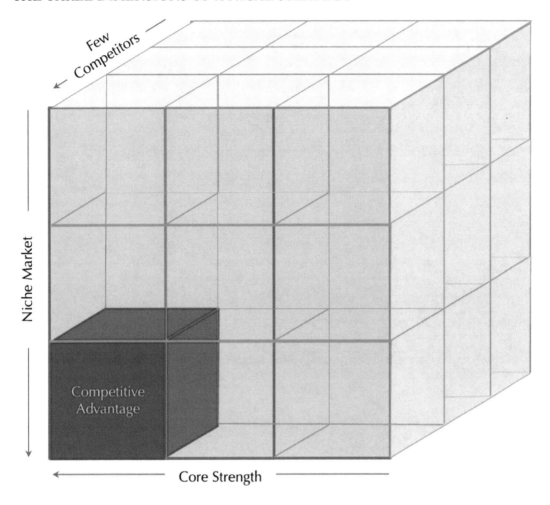

It is a very powerful statement to say, *"We're the only company that..."* There are many ways you can leverage your current strengths and make this statement about your company. The Holy Grail is when you can say, *"We are the only company that provides this product/service in this industry in this geography and provides this type of guarantee"*.

Some entrepreneurs have difficulty creating niche strategies because they are trying to be everything to everyone. They are thinking about their business too opportunistically. If this is you, you will need to eliminate this mindset. To help you understand how to make this happen in your business, read through these real world examples. These examples show you how some of our clients have created winning niche strategies.

Magazine Publishing Industry

The publishing industry has been declining over the past decade based on disruptive market forces (the Internet) and recessionary economics (decreased advertising spend). So can a magazine publishing company defy these odds and qualify as one of the fastest growing companies in the US?

Yes, N2 Publishing is a perfect example. N2 Publishing created a niche strategy by producing high-quality neighborhood magazines for affluent communities. These magazines provide companies a very targeted advertising medium at an affordable price point. There is some overhead to produce these magazines, but it's fairly low because the content is free (it's written by the community residents).

After developing the business in Wilmington, N.C., the owners have now replicated the model in over 100 cities. Their niche strategy is unique because:

- N2 Publishing is the only nationwide company producing neighborhood magazines (Unique product with few competitors)

- N2 Publishing focuses on very specific target markets — affluent neighborhoods and the businesses who want to advertise to these neighborhoods


Fundraising Industry

There are many companies offering products and services to non-profit organizations to support fundraising efforts. You are probably familiar with many of these products such as cookies, popcorn, candy bars, magazines, and coupon discounts. Breaking through this clutter can be difficult for non-profits and requires a significant effort to raise even small dollars.

Brax, Ltd. observed this challenge for non-profits and created a unique product that separates itself from the "traditional" fundraising products. The product is a unique "Spirit Cup" that includes a 3D design of professional and college team logos. Sports fans love the cups and can only buy these cups through non-profit organizations. In most cases, these non-profits include youth sports teams who are raising money.

Brax, Ltd. created a winning niche strategy by developing a unique product (Spirit Cup) focused on a specific target market (youth sports teams) and leveraged the owners' passion for helping others.

## Freight Transportation Industry

One of the hardest hit industries during the 2008-09 recession was the freight transportation industry because of decreased demand. Transportation providers and freight brokers saw their revenue decline sharply and many of these companies went out of business. While this was occurring, a small freight broker, LoadMatch Logistics, implemented a niche strategy that resulted in significant revenue growth.

The founders of LoadMatch Logistics observed an industry challenge where importers paid for two-way truck shipments even though they only needed one-way. Importers paid not only for product delivery but also for the empty return to the port. LoadMatch solved this challenge by creating a database and process that matched import freight with outbound export freight. LoadMatch passed the bulk of the transportation savings to the customers.

By solving an industry challenge (empty loads) and focusing on a specific market (U.S. Exporters), LoadMatch created a competitive advantage. This advantage allowed LoadMatch to grow revenue exponentially.

## Consumer Discount Industry

The consumer discount industry has become a crowded space with companies like Groupon and Living Social. In addition to the latest Internet discount business models, there are many companies that sell coupon books through non-profits to raise money. While coupon books provide a local competitive advantage, the model does not leverage the Internet and requires consumers to carry around a bulky book.

After identifying this challenge in the marketplace, Frank Deals launched a consumer discount card that provides the same local focus, but also leverages the Internet. Consumers carry a card in their wallet versus a bulky coupon book and can find deals using Internet browsers or smart phones. In addition, merchants using the card can offer daily discounts to Frank Card Members. The card allows merchants to track marketing campaigns and customer loyalty — a key feature not provided with a traditional coupon book.

Frank Deals sells the cards the same way many coupon books do. The distribution channel includes mostly schools and non-profit organizations. What's different about the card is that instead of a one-time purchase, card members renew their card each year online. This creates an annuity stream for the non-profit that originally sold the card.

Frank Deals leveraged the Internet to disrupt the traditional coupon book business model. Frank Deals offers a better service to consumers, non-profits and merchants — a niche strategy that has allowed it to take significant market share from an embedded competitor.

Frozen Yogurt Industry

In 2006, a new type of frozen yogurt restaurant model began making waves across the country. This new model included self-service and a buffet bar of toppings. Three young entrepreneurs who just graduated from college recognized this trend while traveling to different cities. The entrepreneurs also knew this trend had not yet arrived in Wilmington, N.C.

After studying other frozen yogurt restaurants, the entrepreneurs replicated the business model of a wildly popular franchise and launched Fuzzy Peach — the first self-service yogurt bar in Southeastern North Carolina. The model proved profitable and the entrepreneurs re-invested the profits to open an additional four locations (As of publication, several more franchises are in the works.).

Fuzzy Peach is a great example of re-purposing a niche strategy in a new market.

<u>Training Industry</u>

If you Google "Training Consultants", "Training Providers" or "Instructional Design," you will find hundreds, if not thousands, of companies that provide training services.  If you want to differentiate yourself from this vast number of competitors, you need to demonstrate both competency and industry expertise.  Proficient Learning did just that by developing an offering focused on specialty sales training in the pharmaceutical industry.

The founder of Proficient Learning had a background as a training director and realized very few companies focused on this particular niche — Pharmaceutical Specialty Sales Training.  Consequently, most providers failed to meet the expectations of pharmaceutical companies.  With a passion for training, the founder launched Proficient Learning to solve this challenge in the marketplace.

Proficient Learning's niche strategy has enabled it to win opportunities when competing against much larger competitors because of its expertise and core focus.

## Create Your Niche

If you don't already have a winning niche strategy, the examples in this book demonstrate that it's not that difficult to create one.  The biggest roadblock is probably your mindset because the best niche strategy may mean disrupting your current business model.  You may need to think outside of the box and leverage ideas outside of your current industry or geography.

To create your winning niche strategy, you may find it helpful to:

1. Identify challenges in your industry and target market. Evaluate the best solutions to solve these challenges. If you have the resources and expertise to solve this challenge, you have likely found your niche.

2. Travel to different cities and explore how companies in your industry are competing and marketing their service or product.

3. Attend trade shows and conferences. Remove yourself from day to day operations and take time to strategically think about your business.

4. Explore new trends in different industries and brainstorm ways these trends can be applied to your business, industry and target market.

5. Test market potential niche strategies. If you can easily sell the solution or product, you are on to something.

6. Re-invent your business model using the latest technology or resources (if you don't do it, a competitor likely will).

7. Create a mastermind group or join a Peer Advisory Board offered through organizations like The Alternative Board®. Get input from others outside of your business as you may be too close to the problem.

8. Facilitate brainstorming sessions with your employees and customers. Your best idea may come from someone inside your company or a customer you currently serve.

9. Be open to failure. Some of the best-known entrepreneurs have tried a dozen different business ideas before being successful.

10. Execute on your ideas and stay committed during the test pilot. In many cases the problem isn't the idea, it's poor leadership or lack of accountability / planning.

11. Explore ways to differentiate your current product or service. This may include a customer service commitment (i.e., 30 minutes or less or your pizza is free), a warranty (i.e., 10 year warranty or free follow up service

calls) or a differentiated product or service feature.

## **The Absence of a Niche Strategy**

Without a Unique Value Proposition (UVP), you will have to put forth more effort to grow revenue. This will include developing better relationships, implementing the best marketing/advertising programs, building your brand (reputation), delivering excellent customer service and increasing operational efficiency (price competitiveness). If you are well capitalized and have solid management practices, this may be doable. Community banks and independent insurance agencies are a perfect example on how this can be done. It's very difficult to differentiate your company on interest/insurance rates and service fees. Small banks and insurance agencies win market share through relationships, individual sales skills and customer service.

If you don't have an effective niche strategy, you will definitely need the best people, culture and management systems to win in the marketplace. The goal of this book and our coaching program is to help you develop a competitive advantage (niche strategy) combined with the best execution (people and process).

# CHAPTER 5

# PEOPLE MANAGEMENT

Both business owners and employees desire a workplace culture that not only supports a rewarding work environment, but also encourages high performance. While this goal is ubiquitous, the management practices and leadership traits required to achieve this goal are not always understood or implemented with consistency.

Creating the right workplace culture for your company is not complex, but does require discipline and changing old habits. This discipline requires company leadership to implement six management practices:

1. Create a company vision shared by all.

2. Develop an accountability chart (identify the right seats).

3. Establish both performance and behavior expectations (match the right people to the right seats — Performance Values Matrix).

4. Develop 90-Day company plans (goals, company priorities and action plans).

5. Facilitate weekly leadership meetings.

6. Schedule team-building activities.

Implementing these six practices will reward high performers and team players. It will provide a workplace where expectations are known and employee contributions are appreciated. Customer service will improve (Research has shown employees provide better customer service when they enjoy their work.). Leaders will feel comfortable delegating tasks and not feel compelled to micro-manage. Your organization will be aligned with a common purpose. Candid communication will identify issues before major problems arise. And last, but not least, you will work less and the company will grow without your day-to-day operational involvement.

## **A Company Vision & Mission Shared by All**

Your company vision and mission are the foundation of your company's core values and the cornerstone of your workplace culture. Your mission establishes the purpose of your organization while your vision clarifies your future direction. When establishing your mission you may want to consider answering these four questions:

1. Why should a customer purchase your product or service?

    a. Why is your company, product and service unique?

2. Why should employees work for you?

3. Why should your community support you?

4. What returns do your owners / investors require?

Your vision should clarify:

1. The products and services you will deliver in the future (Will we add something new? Will we improve (innovate) our products or services? Will we stop doing something we're doing now?).

2. The target markets you will serve. This includes the types of customers you

would like to have and the geographies you would like to serve or operate in.

3. What will your future organizational structure look like? For example, the types of positions you will need and/or the number of employees you will need.

A well thought out vision statement will create excitement within your team because it not only identifies opportunities for your organization to grow, but also growth opportunities for your employees.

After you create your company vision and mission, you should share them with everyone and embed them in everything you do as an organization. As your company evolves, your vision should too. Each year when you prepare your overall annual plan, you should test the vision to make sure it's still relevant and on target with the company's direction. If you need to revise, do so and communicate the revisions with the "why" to your entire team.

To embed your company vision and mission in your workplace culture, make sure:

- The vision and mission are communicated during the employee recruiting process and reinforced when the employee on-boards.

- Annual planning sessions begin with reviewing and testing the company vision and mission.

- 90-day planning sessions compare the company's performance to the company vision.

- Employee job descriptions and employee evaluations include the company vision and mission.

## Accountability Chart

Author Jim Collins best describes organizational effectiveness as having the right people in the right seats. To implement this principle, leaders should create an accountability chart that maps key functions of your organization. At the fundamental level, there are five key roles: Visionary, Integrator, Sales/Marketing, Operations and Finance/Administration.

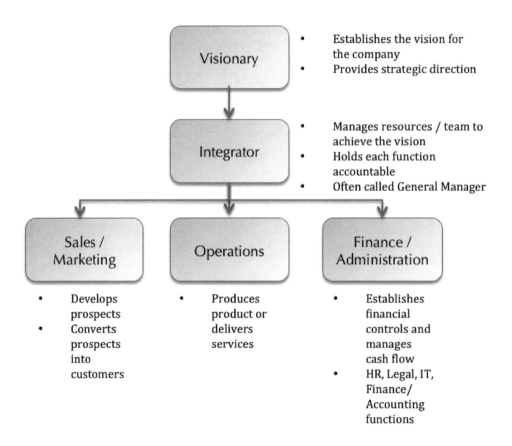

In early-stage companies, a person may fill multiple roles within the accountability chart. As the company grows, it is important to delegate roles and elevate the impact people can have on the company's performance. If a person is micromanaging another employee, this creates more work and is inefficient. Micromanagement is often caused by not letting go, a lack of system/structure/accountability and/or not having the right person in the right seat.

After you create your accountability chart, the next step is to develop the "future state" chart. This chart should reflect what your organization will need to look like to achieve your vision in three to five years. The open seats in your future state will help you understand where you will need to develop employees or recruit new talent. In some cases, you may find you need to add additional functions to your future state chart such as customer service, human resources, and information technology.

When company ownership involves more than one person, the owners should view themselves as "stock holders" in the company and create the accountability chart as if they were the Board of Directors.

One word of caution to consider when developing your accountability chart is to avoid titles such as Director, VP, et cetera. Titles may be important when it comes to customers and suppliers, but titles often create unhealthy politics inside organizations.

## Performance Values Matrix

The Performance Values Matrix is designed to clearly communicate expectations and evaluate employees from two perspectives: Behaviors and Performance. The right behaviors support a positive company culture and develop an atmosphere of trust, teamwork, creativity and candor. Performance definitions communicate expectations and provide a basis for employee feedback. By managing both behaviors and performance, the company will create a performance culture that consistently delivers results and increases workplace satisfaction.

Employees who regularly meet and exceed expectations and demonstrate behaviors consistent with core values are your *star* team members.

Employees who show the right values, but are lacking in performance, are team members with *potential*. If your Potentials have the necessary acumen, you should be able to coach them to become stars as they gain more experience and developmental training.

Employees who are meeting performance expectations, but lack core values, are *misaligned* with your company culture. It will be more difficult to coach Misaligned employees to become Stars, than coaching your Potentials to become Stars, as behaviors are engrained in an employee's personality.

Employees who are failing to meet performance expectations and lack core values may not be the *right fit* because they weigh your company down and keep you stuck in the same place.

You should spend 80% of your management time on your star employees. Identifying your star players will help you create a profile to evaluate potential new hires. Star players should not only be identified for leadership positions, but also be asked to mentor their peers.

Rules of Thumb to Always Remember:

- Managers often hire for experience, knowledge and connections, and usually fire because of behaviors. Behaviors should be a key part of your interview evaluation process.

- Managers often hire quickly, but fire slowly. Recruiting should be treated like sales. Always prospect for good employees. Don't wait until the last minute to recruit new employees.

- While it is difficult to terminate someone, your culture and productivity will improve after firing an employee that does not display your core values. In most cases, you will ask yourself, "Why didn't I do that sooner?"

# PERFORMANCE VALUES MATRIX

**Performance / Goal Attainment** (vertical axis) | **Behaviors / Attitude / Culture Fit** (horizontal axis)

### Misalignment (top-left)
- Employee is achieving goals, but is displaying behaviors / attitudes that do not support the company culture and may be negatively affecting the team.
- Coaching should focus on changing behaviors / attitude.
- It is usually more difficult to coach behaviors than performance -- You may find it beneficial to utilize a DISC Behavioral Assessment.

### Stars (top-right)
- Employee is achieving desired performance and is a great team player.
- Coaching should focus on career advancement and continuous improvement.
- Potentially a mentor for other team members.
- It's important to help Star employees achieve their personal vision.

### Right Fit? (bottom-left)
- Employee does not demonstrate the behaviors and attitude to support the company culture; Employee also does not achieve the desired performance level.
- Coaching should focus on rapid improvement in both areas or encouraged to work elsewhere.
- Managers often keep Anchors on the team too long -- Avoid doing this.

### Potential (bottom-right)
- Employee demonstrates required behaviors and attitude, but has not achieved desired performance level.
- Coaching should focus on skills and knowledge.
- Employee will probably become a star if they have the capacity to learn and perform.
- You may want to explore if another position is better suited for the employee.

---

Performance Expectation Examples

Sales

1. Meet sales goal (i.e., by month or quarter).

2. Meet prospect pipeline goal (i.e., number of prospects and financial value of opportunities).

3. Close sales at or above gross profit margin target.

4. Set realistic customer expectations during the sales process

## Marketing

1. Marketing initiatives create qualified prospects (i.e., number of prospects).
2. Support sales business development goals (i.e., number of prospects developed by sales force).
3. Develop annual marketing plans/budget and meet established timelines.

## Customer Service

1. Meet customer satisfaction survey scores.
2. Upsell x% of call-in customers.
3. Develop x number of referrals from customer call-ins.
4. Meet problem resolution time for customers (i.e., close out open tickets in a set time).

## Operations

1. Meet production time schedules.
2. Achieve quality standards.
3. Maintain cost targets.
4. Meet customer satisfaction survey scores.

## Finance

1. Create working capital requirement reports on a monthly basis.
2. Produce financial analysis reports and company scorecards weekly.
3. Manage Accounts Receivable (i.e., DSO and Bad Debt).
4. Manage Accounts Payable (i.e., avoid late payments unless cash flow constrained).

Expectations for Workplace Behaviors

After creating the performance expectations, you will need to create the behaviors that support your core values. The Performance Values Matrix includes 12 behaviors commonly found in high performance teams, including:

1. Quality Orientation
2. Work Ethic
3. Leadership
4. Adaptability
5. Communication
6. Candor
7. Judgment/Problem Solving
8. Initiative
9. Teamwork
10. Reliability
11. Stress Tolerance
12. Planning/Organization

Once 2 x 2's are created for each position, managers should explain to each team member how performance and behaviors will be evaluated. Managers are also encouraged to use the 2 x 2's as part of the evaluation process when interviewing potential new hires.

It's important to also include a job description in the Performance Values Matrix. The job description should describe responsibilities, reporting relationships and compensation (if a formula is used to calculate bonuses and/or commissions).

## Employee Performance & Behavior Expectations (Example)

Employee Name: John Smith  Manager: Harry Wallace
Job Role: General Manager  Date: 6/1/14

| | Performance Criteria | Rating | Weighting | Score |
|---|---|---|---|---|
| 1 | Revenue & Profit Goals | 1 | 25.0% | 0.25 |
| 2 | Employee Performance | 2 | 25.0% | 0.50 |
| 3 | Traction -- 90 Day Plans; Issue Resolution & Acco | 1.5 | 25.0% | 0.38 |
| 4 | Scalability (Process & Delegation) | 1 | 25.0% | 0.25 |
| | | | 100% | 1.38 |

| | Cultural Values / Key Behaviors | Rating | Weighting | |
|---|---|---|---|---|
| 1 | Quality Orientation | 1 | 8.3% | 0.08 |
| 2 | Work Ethic | 2 | 8.3% | 0.17 |
| 3 | Leadership | 1.5 | 8.3% | 0.13 |
| 4 | Adaptability | 1 | 8.3% | 0.08 |
| 5 | Communication Style | 1 | 8.3% | 0.08 |
| 6 | Trustworthiness | 1 | 8.3% | 0.08 |
| 7 | Judgment / Problem Solving / Decision Making | 1.5 | 8.3% | 0.13 |
| 8 | Initiative | 1 | 8.3% | 0.08 |
| 9 | Teamwork | 1 | 8.3% | 0.08 |
| 10 | Reliability | 1 | 8.3% | 0.08 |
| 11 | Stress Tolerance | 1.5 | 8.3% | 0.13 |
| 12 | Planning / Organization | 1 | 8.3% | 0.08 |
| | Cultural / Behavior Score | | 100% | 1.21 |

Rating Footnotes
- 2 Exceeds Expectations Frequently
- 1.5 Exceeds Expectations Some Times
- 1 Meets Expectations All The Time
- 0.5 Meets Expectations Some Times
- 0 Underperforming / Below Expectations

# Employee Performance & Behavior Expectations (Page 2 Example)

**Manager's Notes:**
**Professional Development Goals**
Complete the Industry Certification Program

**Evaluation**
Great job meeting sales forecast
Organizing shows, ordering materials, keeping track of calendar has been good
Accessibility to talking to reps on nights and weekends
Great internal resource for reps
**Improvement areas:**
Develop a leader within the Wilmington office
Keeping track of reports( Top 120 accounts, Open FR analysis)

Employee Signature: _____ Date: _____

(Employee acknowledges the Manager has reviewed this evaluation with him/her.)

Manager's Signature: _____ Date: _____

## Team Performance Values Matrix Example

Once all employees ratings have been completed, you can plot team members on a Performance Values Matrix.

The team Performance Values Matrix not only provides insight on how your organization is performing overall, but also highlights areas that need development.

## 90-day Plan

A 90-day plan prioritizes the most important company initiatives and provides a clear direction for your team. 90-day plans break your annual goals into quarterly segments and makes it easier to understand the critical success factors, strategies and action plans necessary to achieve your ultimate objectives. The 90-Day Planning Session Agenda should include:

1. Company Vision and Mission.
2. Last Quarter Performance Review.
3. Goals for the Next 90 Days.
4. Three to Five Critical Success Factors.
5. Strategies and Action Plans to Achieve the Critical Success Factors (use the S.M.A.R.T. principle):
    a. Specific
    b. Measurable
    c. Attainable
    d. Responsible Person (always select one lead)
    e. Timeline

A facilitator guide for the 90-Day Planning Session is located in the Business Coach's Toolbox (Chapter 9).

## Weekly Leadership Meetings

Weekly leadership meetings are designed to provide a forum where department leaders collaborate with each other in an open, candid environment. Providing a weekly checkpoint enables the team to quickly identify issues and create action plans to resolve the issues. The meeting provides more efficient communication as topics/issues that can wait for the meeting are handled during this time (versus constant, daily interruptions). It also encourages department leaders to work together as a team to improve each department's performance.

The meeting should not last longer than 90 minutes. Placing a timeline on the meeting will force the team to prioritize issues and resolve them efficiently. If the meeting agenda can be accomplished in less time, end early (avoid adding fillers or extending the meeting to fit the time). Most companies can complete the majority of meetings in 45 minutes or less.

The meeting agenda should include:

1. Best Thing (1 business/1 personal). 5 to 10 minutes. Purpose is to start the meeting off on the right note. Avoid tangents.

2. Company News. 5 to 10 minutes. Share important client, employee, supplier or industry news.

3. Department Scorecard. 5 minutes  Department leads share their KPI performance for the previous week. If a KPI falls below expectations, add to the issue list.

4. Action Plan Review. 5 to 10 minutes. Department leads provide a status update on action plans (On-Track or Off-Track). If off-track, add this to the issue list and avoid diving in until all issues have been prioritized.

5. Issues. 10 to 65 minutes. If department leads have issues/action plans that need input, they are put on the table for discussion. The meeting facilitator, usually the integrator, prioritizes the issues and opens up for discussion (It is important to avoid tangent conversations that don't solve the issue.). The team creates action plans to solve the issue. The integrator adds the action plans to the next week's meeting agenda.

6. Meeting Wrap-Up. 5 minutes. The integrator summarizes action plans and adds assignments to the next week's meeting agenda.

## Schedule Team Building Activities

The best performing companies we coach have both formal and informal company gatherings to promote goodwill and friendships. In a way, the outings are designed to reward employees for their hard work and dedication. I've seen increased workplace satisfaction and better customer service when employees have friends inside the company because the company becomes more than just a place to earn a salary. The intrinsic reward of friendships motivates employees to be team players and push harder to meet team goals. Friendships also increase the level of trust inside an organization and decrease employee turnover.

The team-building activities can be as simple as company lunches, Friday afternoon cookouts or a night at the bowling alley.

## Change Management

If your company has a history of departments working in silos, department leads may initially find the weekly pulse meetings a waste of time – i.e., "This issue has nothing to do with my department and I need to get back to my department". This departmental mindset will prevent your company from truly excelling and limit your company's ability to develop creative solutions that can deliver significant business value. Effective managers not only care about their department, but also the company overall and the performance of their peers. In addition to creative problem solving, the meetings provide a forum for peer accountability and ensure alignment regarding company initiatives and action plans.

## Competitive Advantage - The Human Element

Internet-based applications have made it easy for entrepreneurs to duplicate systems and processes that once differentiated larger companies. However, this sword has a double edge — it's easy for your competitors to do the same. To separate yourself from your competitors, leaders should focus on the human element. If you hire right and develop a strong culture, your team will ultimately win. Jim Collins research has proven this year after year.

# CHAPTER 6
# PROCESS EXCELLENCE

Magic happens when an entrepreneur combines creativity with effective people management and process excellence. However, if you are like many entrepreneurs we coach, you cringe at the thought of process management. Entrepreneurs are the "idea guys" and are most likely good with people, but when it comes to process, it's a different game all together.

If this statement resonates with you, there is good news. Process does not have to be extremely complicated or mundane. I'm a firm believer in Pareto's Law — doing 20% of the effort can produce 80% of the benefit. Process management can also be easily delegated.

During numerous coaching sessions, I have illustrated this point while working through a client's business challenge. As a client begins to discuss a challenge, I ask him or her to use the white board to walk me through the process related to the challenge. In less than an hour, two things typically happen. One is clarity and the other is process improvement. Clarity helps the entrepreneur understand the root cause of the challenge and helps us identify solutions that may involve personnel change/training, process re-design or new technology. Process not only helps you identify solutions for improvement, but also creates a platform that delivers quality, consistency, efficiency and scalability.

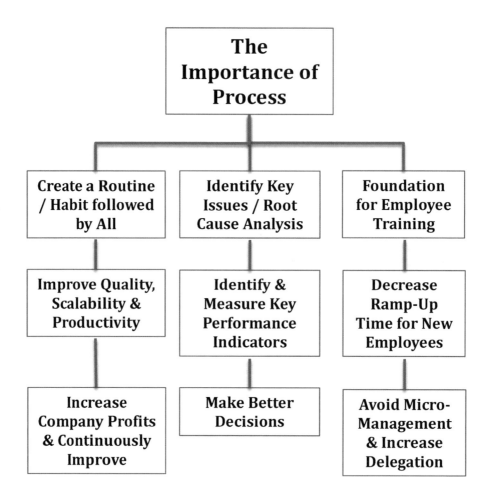

Quality & Consistency

With a documented process, you have a standard for your employees to follow. Following a process ensures the same results are achieved time after time. The outcome is not dependent on the employees skill set or acumen, although you do have to make sure an employee has the ability to follow the process and be intuitive enough to provide suggestions for improvement.

## Efficiency

Processes not only improve production efficiency, but also decrease the time it takes to on-board new employees. Documented processes provide a basis for training new employees. Without this documentation it takes longer for new employees to learn and requires another individual to spend more time training the new hire.

## Scalability

Processes create systems that can be managed without the day-to-day involvement from business owners or key leaders. This is one reason why many franchise systems have been so successful. The franchisor has documented a proven way to operate and provides franchisees a play book to execute.

The 10x companies described in Jim Collins' book <u>Great by Choice</u> outperformed their competition because of their ability to scale. The ability to scale is more important than the ability to innovate. Scalability requires a well-defined process that is easily repeatable.

## Delegation

Micro-management is a common problem in many organizations. One of the root causes of micromanagement is the lack of process documentation. If you have a process that clearly documents tasks and responsibilities, a manager should not have to micromanage unless they have the wrong person in the seat.

We have found it fairly easy to delegate the process management to functional leads. Functional leads are asked to identify the most common processes and document the key steps in each process.

## Technology / Applications

Fortunately, most applications used today have built-in user help functions and tutorials so there is no need to document all the details for each process. Just make sure you highlight the primary steps and notate the person responsible and the application used to support the process. For example, Customer Relationship Management (CRM) applications support your sales and customer service processes.

## Define Your Value Chain

To manage your processes and build a platform for continuous improvement, you will find it helpful to document the key processes to acquire customers and deliver value. We call this your Value Chain.

Each section of your value chain should include Key Performance Indicators (KPIs). Your KPIs will be financial and operational metrics that gauge your company's performance. These metrics will help you identify potential issues/challenges before real problems arise. Leaders will make better decisions over the long run by using data versus hunches. KPIs are often referred to as a Scorecard or Executive Dashboard.

## Value Chain Example

| Lead Generation | Need Identification | Solution Development | Service Delivery | Customer Care |
|---|---|---|---|---|

### KEY ACTIVITIES

| Lead Generation | Need Identification | Solution Development | Service Delivery | Customer Care |
|---|---|---|---|---|
| • Events<br>• Advertising<br>• Business Development<br>• Press<br>• Referrals<br>• Customer Base | • Identify challenge / need<br>• Budget, Timeframe, Decision Makers, Key Influencers<br>• Concerns<br>• Determine fit | • Develop solution based on needs<br>• Quality Assurance / Risk Assessment<br>• Price solution<br>• Contract negotiation<br>• Close opportunity | • Implement transition plan<br>• Manage budget and delivery resources<br>• Weekly checkpoint calls<br>• Deliverable approvals | • Customer Survey<br>• Post delivery customer support |

### KEY PERFORMANCE INDICATORS

| Lead Generation | Need Identification | Solution Development | Service Delivery | Customer Care |
|---|---|---|---|---|
| Marketing ROI Metrics | $ Value of Qualified Opportunities | $ Value of Booked Opportunities | Gross Profit | Customer Survey |
| # of Pre-Qualified Opportunities | # of Qualified Opportunities | Development Cost & Profit Forecast | Resource Utilization | Customer Retention |
|  |  | Close Ratio |  |  |

## Company Scorecard

The purpose of a Scorecard is to provide you and your leadership team a summary of your company performance and current condition. The KPIs identified in your Value Chain will be incorporated into your Scorecard as well as important financial data and ratios. With a Scorecard in place you can quickly ascertain what is going on in your business. The scorecard will help you make better decisions and allow you to spend more time on other activities. These activities can include strategic initiatives or interests outside of work.

You Scorecard should reflect your company's key economic drivers. Some of these drivers will be unique to your industry while others will be common financial metrics. If you need help identifying KPIs for your industry, you can visit www.kpilibrary.com. The KPI Library contains over 6,500 KPIs categorized by industry and function.

If you need help identifying and understanding common financial metrics and ratios, you may want to look at a ProfitCents report. Your accountant or business coach will probably have access to these reports. ProfitCents reports are helpful because the data is based on privately held companies, company size (revenue) and industry. The reports will also provide an opportunity for you to benchmark your performance against your peers.

## Company Scorecard Example

**Month:** January, 2012

|  | GOAL | ACTUAL |
|---|---|---|
| **Key Financial Metrics** |  |  |
| Monthly Sales | $100K | $94K |
| Gross Profit Margin | 50% | 45% |
| Net Profit Margin | 10% | 9% |
|  |  |  |
| Working Capital (Cash) | $60K | $63K |
| Accounts Receivable (AR) | $120K | $110K |
| Total Current Assets | $180K | $173K |
| AR passed 90 Days | $0K | $9K |
|  |  |  |
| Accounts Payable | $30K | $25K |
| Other Current Liabilities (Salaries, Rent, etc.) | $60K | $62K |
| Total Current Liabilities | $90K | $87K |
|  |  |  |
| Current Ratio | 2.0 | 1.99 |
|  |  |  |
| Work in Progress (Booked Projects) | $125K | $150K |
| **Key Sales & Marketing Metrics** |  |  |
| Cost / Lead | $350 | $425 |
| Close Rate | 33% | 27% |
| Pipeline ($ Value of Qualified Opportunities) | $400K | $250K |
| Annual Sales / Customer | $25K | $18K |
| Customer Attrition | 5% | 7% |
| Customer Satisfaction Score (Scale 1.0 to 5.0) | 4.5 | 4.7 |
|  |  |  |
| **Key Operation Metrics** |  |  |
| Utilization Rate (Hours Worked / Hours Available) | 75% | 72% |
| Sales / Employee | $225K | $202K |
| Employee Attrition | 10% | 0% |

## Process Management

After defining your Value Chain you will have a good idea of the processes you should manage. To manage these processes you will first need to document the key steps, tools used and person(s) responsible. The documentation will become part of your company playbook and will be utilized for training and continuous improvement. Core processes will typically include:

1. Marketing
2. Sales
3. Operations/Customer Fulfillment/Manufacturing - (Depending on your industry, you are likely to have multiple sub-categories under operations.)
4. Customer Service
5. Human Resources
    a. Recruiting, Employee Reviews and Termination/Separation
6. Finance & Accounting
    a. Accounts Receivable
    b. Purchase Orders/Accounts Payable
    c. Payroll
    d. Inventory Management
    e. Taxes (Sales, Corporate, Payroll)
    f. Budgeting and Reporting

After developing a list of your core business functions, you can use the Performance Culture Process Template to document the key steps, tasks, tools used, persons responsible and time required/expected. In the appendix section you will find an example of a company's playbook — a collection of documented processes.

Example: Sales Process

| STEP | TASK | ROLE | TOOLS USED | TIME FRAME |
|---|---|---|---|---|
| 1 | Research target market and create prospect list | Business Advisor | Prospect Template / Sales Plan | Completed on a monthly basis |
| 2 | Develop trusted relationships with prospects before trying to sell<br>• Show genuine interest in person and company<br>• Demonstrate industry acumen -- Build credibility | BA | Phone calls, In person visits, Company Sales Collateral; CRM App | Daily |
| 3 | Identify needs & Qualify prospects<br>• Ask probing questions to identify needs, wants, concerns and pending events<br>• Understand the decision making process, timeline and budget | BA | Prospect Questionnaire Template (MS Word); CRM App | Completed within 30 days of developing prospect relationship |
| 4 | Develop solution<br>• Demonstrate ROI / benefit for customer<br>• Reinforce our uniqueness in this space | BA | Indicative Solution Presentation (MS PowerPoint); CRM App | Completed within 2 weeks after qualifying prospect |
| 5 | Close<br>• Deliver proposal and close<br>• Gain verbal agreement before sending formal proposal | BA | Company Proposal Template (MS Word); CRM App | Time Frame determined during qualification step |
| 6 | Customer Survey<br>• Conduct customer satisfaction survey on phone<br>• Document customer testimonial | BA | Customer Survey Template; CRM App | Completed one week after 1st deliverable is given to customer |

Case Study: An Example of Process Excellence in Sales

A business owner in media industry noticed that one of his Account Executives (AE) was consistently outselling the rest of the team. During a coaching session, the owner asked me why I thought there was such a difference. The star AE had similar clients, sold the same advertising packages and displayed similar behaviors as the other AEs. I suggested we schedule a team meeting to explore the company's sales process.

Once we gathered the team, I asked each AE to write down the steps each person took to find prospects, build trust & rapport, identify & qualify opportunities, propose solutions and close sales. This exercise quickly identified the root cause of the problem – each AE used a different process to sell. To address the problem we documented the sales process the star employee was using and discussed the key techniques employed in each step of the process.

The documented process created a "proven way" to sell advertising and provided a platform to consistently measure the sales process. The underperforming AEs became high performers by implementing the same process and techniques used by the star employee. When new AE's are hired, the sales manager now trains the new employees using the documented sales process. This training has significantly reduced the time it takes for a new hire to meet or exceed his/her sales quota.

# CHAPTER 7
# SUCCESSION PLANNING & EXIT STRATEGIES

If you envision executing an exit strategy or a succession plan in five years or less, the time to plan is now. Obviously you want to maximize your business value and create financial security as part of your succession plan. Creating a business that can grow without your day-to-day involvement will help maximize your business value.

Implementing the Performance Culture System will help you accomplish this and will offer you attractive exit strategy options. Once your business can earn and grow profits without your day-to-day involvement, you have an option to create a dividend stream from your own company or sell it at an attractive multiple.

Creating an effective succession plan or exit strategy will include a buy/sell agreement, key man insurance, equity transfer or purchase subscription agreement, tax planning and wealth management. You will need the appropriate professionals (i.e., attorney, financial advisor and accountant) to create these components of your plan. Your successor can be an employee, family member or new hire that has the potential to manage and grow your business without your operational involvement.

NOTE: You and your successor should complete his or her leadership development plan and should demonstrate effective leadership before you create legal documents and equity agreements.

Selecting your successor and transitioning your leadership responsibilities are where the Performance Culture System comes into place. The ultimate objective is to achieve your personal vision. To accomplish this, you will need to have the right incentives and company controls in place. Successful succession plans will give you an option to earn continuous dividends as well as receive a nice pay-out when the business sells (if that is part of your personal vision). It will also align your personal vision with the goals of your successor.

There are five key steps to prepare your succession plan:

Step One: Vision & Mission

- Create your personal vision. If multiple owners are involved, you will need to make sure there is alignment among all equity holders. (See Personal Vision Template)

- Create a company vision and mission that enables you to achieve your personal vision. (See Company Vision & Mission Template)

- Make sure your company vision and mission are shared by all.

Step Two: Define your Company's Critical Success Factors (see Company Foundation Template)

- Define your leadership role. Describe the key skills, knowledge and relationships required to manage and grow your company.

- Create your company's accountability chart. Identify the roles and responsibilities necessary to achieve your company vision.

- Assess your team's effectiveness using the Performance Values Matrix. Identify gaps and employee underperformance. Identify potential successors.

- Assess your company's strengths and weaknesses. What must be improved to ensure the company's longevity?

- Define three to five Critical Success Factors to grow profits and ensure company sustainability.

Step Three:  Select the Successor

- After identifying your potential successors, evaluate them using the leadership effectiveness framework (see Leadership Effectiveness Template):
    - Have they earned the will of their team, clients and partners?
    - Do they communicate clearly and wisely?
    - Do they hold team members accountable for results?
- Select your Successor (Note:  It is important to avoid selecting someone just because they are most like you; the best leaders we coach all have different styles.)

Step Four:  Create a Professional Development Plan

- Identify key skills, knowledge and relationships the new leader will need in order to be successful and develop a professional development plan accordingly.
- Consider hiring a leadership coach to help with professional development.  A third party perspective can have a significant impact if the right coach is hired.

Step Five:  Implement the Performance Culture System

- Implementing the Performance Culture System will give the owners the assurance they need that the company will continue to grow and earn profits in their absence.

- The Performance Culture System provides this assurance by creating structure, governance, measurements and accountability. The weekly scorecard can be used to brief the owners on company performance, key issues and future action plans on an as needed basis.

- Identify Change Agents and Mavericks (see Employee 2 x 2 Evaluations):
  - Change Agents will be your star employees and will most likely support the leadership transition plan.
  - Mavericks are likely to create resistance and potentially sabotage the leadership succession plan. Their behaviors must be modified or their employment terminated.

Step Six: Develop Your Exit Strategy

After your new leader is leading your business without your day-to-day operational involvement, it is appropriate to explore exit strategy options. Your company's success will depend on the new leader so you will need to provide an incentive that motivates the leader to both grow the business and explore exit strategies that may involve a business sale. Potential incentives include profit sharing, phantom stock and equity transfer.

Profit sharing alone is an incentive to grow profits, but does not motivate the leader in the event of a business sale. Ideally, you either provide the leader an option of purchasing equity with the compensation he/she receives as part of profit sharing or grant phantom stock options. Phantom stock options do not transfer equity, but will allow the leader to benefit from selling the business. For example, if you provide a 20% phantom stock option and the business is sold for $5,000,000, the leader will receive 20% of the proceeds ($1,000,000).

If you have decided to allow the new leader to purchase equity with compensation from profit sharing, you have created a way to monetize your business value. You can also create an Employee Stock Ownership Program (ESOP) to accomplish the same goal. ESOPs are attractive because the income tax savings can be used to purchase the owner's equity, allowing the owner to maintain company control (The owner is usually the Manager of the ESOP Trust.).

Once you and the new leader agree on the best way to share profits and/or transfer equity, you should consult with the appropriate legal, accounting and wealth management professionals to execute the plan. Consulting with a tax attorney and accountant is definitely recommended because there are several methods to maximize your after-tax income. However, if you do this before creating your leadership succession plan, you will most likely run in circles and potentially pay more in professional fees.

Maximize Your Business Value

With your new leader in place, you have already accomplished a key element to maximize your business value. Another benefit is you will probably not be required to stay on after the business is sold – a common condition in business acquisitions where the owner is a key man in the business. Another key element to maximize your business value is to develop capabilities and assets that are seen as strategic to potential acquirers. The Niche Strategy of the Performance Culture System will help you develop these strategic assets.

Companies in desirable industries with discretionary income of $1,000,000 or more should command a valuation multiple of four to five times earnings if they properly prepared for sale. Discretionary income is calculated by adding owner's discretionary expenses to the profit reported on your income statement. Usually amortization and depreciation are also added to the net profit. If you have a strategic acquirer, your multiple will likely be much higher than five. Strategic value can derive from unique capabilities, intellectual capital (i.e., patents), brand reputation / recognition, customers, geographic markets and/or proprietary products and services.

## Find an Acquirer

Your negotiating position will improve if a potential acquirer finds you. Frequent press releases discussing your strategic assets will help make this happen. You can also engage a third party to explore potential synergies through acquisitions. We encourage third party facilitation to maintain confidentiality as well as improve your ability to negotiate a win/win outcome.

# CHAPTER 8
# CONCLUSION & NEXT STEPS

As a business owner and as a person who invests in small companies, I understand the challenges and rewards of entrepreneurism. Managing a business is not easy and there is always something new and unexpected you have to deal with. For entrepreneurs, the highs are higher and the lows are lower. At times it can be lonely and the pressure can be unbelievable. The secret to success is being able to lead through chaos.

When you are successful, your success not only impacts you and your family, but also your employees, clients and community. I am proud of your contribution and know first-hand how hard you work to make it happen every day. Performance Culture will make your job as a business leader easier and more rewarding!

Next Steps

You can implement the Performance Culture System two different ways:

1. Guided Implementation
2. Self Implementation

Guided Implementation

A Performance Culture Coach™ can guide you through implementation and facilitate the planning exercises and management team meetings. This includes both One-on-One and Team Business Coaching.

Our firm has implemented the Performance Culture methods with more than a hundred clients. This experience helps us identify potential obstacles and create action plans to address these obstacles. Questions will arise during implementation and it is helpful to have a Business Coach who can walk you through the process.

To complement the guided implementation, many of our clients also participate in Peer Advisory Boards organized by The Alternative Board® (TAB). The Peer Advisory Boards are comprised of non-competing business owners who help each other by leveraging each board member's experience, knowledge and connections. If you join an existing TAB Peer Advisory Board facilitated by our firm, you are likely to join a group of business owners who have already implemented Performance Culture in their business.

Self-Implementation

If you are a business owner who would like to implement the Performance Culture System without a business coach, you can download the templates found in the next chapter: Coach's Toolbox. The templates are in MS PowerPoint and MS Excel and can be found on our website: PerformanceCulture.com The templates are complementary.

If you are self-implementing, you can also schedule a two-day Performance Culture Workshop. The workshops are facilitated by one of our Business Coaches and are located in Wilmington, N.C. (a great place for a company retreat).

Performance Culture Works!

The management practices and methods described in Performance Culture have proven to work and will work for you as well. Implementing the Performance Culture System will drive profitability and create a great workplace. Your work/life balance will improve and your managers will become great leaders. All that is required from you is the discipline and commitment to execute the management practices described in the Performance Culture System.

We end this book with the Coach's Toolbox. The toolbox contains templates used to implement the Performance Culture System. The toolbox also includes implementer notes and an example of a Company Playbook.

Thank you for taking the time to read our book. If you have any questions or comments, please contact us via our website: PerformanceCulture.com

# CHAPTER 9
# COACH'S TOOLBOX

This chapter includes templates and implementer notes to help you implement the Performance Culture System in your company.

Toolbox Contents:
1. Personal Vision
2. Company Vision & Mission
3. Company Foundation
    - 3.1. Accountability Chart
    - 3.2. Employee Performance Values Matrix
    - 3.3. Performance Values Team Matrix
    - 3.4. Value Chain
    - 3.5. Scorecard
    - 3.6. Current State Assessment
4. Leadership Effectiveness
5. Niche Strategy / Competitive Advantage
6. Process Excellence
7. 90-Day Plan
8. Weekly Team Meeting Agenda
9. Coaching Engagement Project Plan

**Personal Vision Template**

1. <u>Income</u>

    1.1. What is the annual income you desire?

    1.2. How much do you need at a minimum?

2. <u>Work Role</u>

    2.1. What workplace roles can you fill that provide the most value to the business (roles you enjoy doing)?

    2.2. What roles/activities should you delegate within current cash flow constraints?

    2.3. Once cash flow improves, what roles/activities would you like to delegate?

3. <u>Work / Life Balance</u>

    3.1. How much time off do you want (shorter days, shorter weeks, more vacation)?

4. <u>Personal Goals</u>

    4.1. What personal goals do you have (new house, vacation home, write a book, politics, education)?

5. <u>Family</u>

    5.1. Are you the father, mother, husband, and/or wife you want to be? If not, what would you like to change?

    5.2. What family activities do you want to add or pursue more often?

6. <u>Interests & Hobbies</u>

    6.1. What activities or hobbies do you enjoy?

    6.2. Do you want to pursue new hobbies or activities?

    6.3. How much time would you like to spend enjoying your hobbies or personal interests?

7. <u>Philanthropies</u>

    7.1. What philanthropies would you like to support? What philanthropies are important to you?

8. <u>Physical Well Being</u>

    8.1. Are you satisfied with your physical condition?

    8.2. What would you like to improve?

9. <u>Religion</u>

    9.1. Are you comfortable with your current beliefs? If not, what would you like to change and/or explore?

10. <u>Retirement/Exit Strategy</u>

    10.1. When would you like to retire?

    10.2. How do you plan to monetize your business ownership (succession plan and/or sale of business)?

    10.3. What should you change to increase the likelihood of a successful succession plan or business sale?

After answering the Personal Vision questions, you should make sure your company vision and strategic plans will help you achieve your personal vision.

It is important for your spouse and business partners to develop their own personal vision and then share them with one other. Sharing your vision not only builds trust, but also provides direction for your company vision.

If you have a Key Man in place, a person that could become the company leader, it is important to understand his/her personal vision as well – the first step of building a successful succession plan.

# Company Vision & Mission Template

1. Company Vision

    1.1. Your company vision is an internal statement. It defines where you want your company to be in three, five and/or ten years from today. The vision should include:

    1.1.1. Revenue and profit goals

    1.1.2. Types of customers and target markets you serve

    1.1.3. Types of products and/or services you provide

2. Company Mission

    2.1. Your company mission is an external statement. It defines your company's purpose. The mission statement should answer these four questions:

    2.1.1. Why should customers buy your product and/or service?

    2.1.2. Why should employees want to work at your company?

    2.1.3. Why should a community allow you to operate in its geography?

    2.1.4. Why should investors invest in your company?

3. Vision and Mission Shared by All

    3.1. Once you have finished your vision and mission you should share them with everyone in your company. The vision and mission should be embedded in your strategic planning discussions, weekly leadership team meetings and job descriptions.

## Company Foundation Template

Before assessing your leadership effectiveness, it is important to understand your company foundation. This foundation includes your accountability chart, employee evaluations, value chain and scorecard.

1. Accountability Chart

    1.1. The first step is to create your Accountability Chart to represent how your company operates today. Please reference the People Management chapter in this book before doing so.

    1.2. The next step is to create your Accountability Chart for Tomorrow. It should represent the type of organization you will need to fulfill your three to five year company vision.

    1.3. The gaps between the two charts will show you where you will need to develop talent internally and/or hire externally.

2. 2 x 2 Employee Evaluations

    2.1. The first step is to create 2 x 2 Employee Evaluation grids for each of the owner's direct reports.

    2.2. Once you have completed the 2 x 2s for your leadership team, ask each leader to create 2 x 2s for the employees they manage.

3. 2 x 2 Team Evaluation

    3.1. After all 2 x 2s have been completed, you will find it helpful to plot your entire team on the team 2 x 2 Performance Values Matrix. The matrix will highlight your stars, potential stars, mavericks and anchors.

4. The Company Value Chain

    4.1. Your company Value Chain represents your way of acquiring customers and delivering value. It represents the core of your business model and should be understood by all employees.

# Company Value Chain Template

## KEY ACTIVITIES

- List Activities
- List Activities
- List Activities
- List Activities
- List Activities

## KEY PERFORMANCE INDICATORS

- List Metrics
- List Metrics
- List Metrics
- List Metrics
- List Metrics

5. Company Scorecard (Template)

**Scorecard for:**          **Month:**

|  | GOAL | ACTUAL |
|---|---|---|
| **Key Financial Metrics** (Enter Your Financial Goals) | | |
| Monthly Sales | | |
| Gross Profit Margin | | |
| Net Profit Margin | | |
| | | |
| Working Capital (Cash) | | |
| Accounts Receivable (AR) | | |
| Total Current Assets | | |
| AR passed 90 Days | | |
| | | |
| Accounts Payable | | |
| Other Current Liabilities (Salaries, Rent, etc.) | | |
| Total Current Liabilities | | |
| | | |
| Current Ratio | | |
| | | |
| Work in Progress (Booked Projects) | | |
| | | |
| **Key Sales & Marketing Metrics** (Enter your KPIs Below) | | |
| | | |
| | | |
| | | |
| | | |
| | | |
| | | |
| **Key Operation Metrics** (Enter your KPIs Below) | | |
| | | |
| | | |
| | | |
| | | |
| | | |
| | | |
| | | |

6. Current State Assessment

   6.1. **Marketing**

   6.1.1. Do we need to improve our branding/messaging?

   6.1.2. Do we need to improve advertising/lead generation activities? In what areas? (i.e., online, offline)

   6.1.3. Do we need to improve the marketing ROI?

   6.1.4. Are we tracking lead generation sources effectively?

   6.1.5. Do we need to improve sales collateral?

   6.1.6. Do we need to support a new product launch?

   6.1.7. Do we have everything ready, do we just need to focus on execution?

   6.1.8. What products/services can deliver the highest revenue over the next 90 days?

   6.1.9. What customer segments and/or geographies can deliver the highest revenue over the next 90 days?

   6.2. **Sales**

   6.2.1. Do we need to improve our sales process?

   6.2.2. Do we have a solid sales plan to execute?

   6.2.3. Do we need to improve sales performance in specific areas or overall?

   6.2.4. Are we setting reasonable customer expectations?

   6.3. **Customer Service**

   6.3.1. Are we delivering an exceptional customer experience?

   6.3.2. Are we quickly solving customer issues?

   6.3.3. Do we need to improve our customer service process?

   6.4. **Operations**

   6.4.1. Are our products ready to sell?

   6.4.2. Will we be able to produce enough products to meet the sales quota in a timely manner?

   6.4.3. Are our costs to produce in line with the budget?

   6.4.4. Do we need to improve operational processes?

   6.4.5. Are we consistently producing quality products and/or services?

   6.4.6. Are we fulfilling customer orders with very few errors?

### 6.5. Technology
  6.5.1. Does our technology/applications support our processes?
  6.5.2. Can technology improve our process cost effectively?
  6.5.3. Do we have system downtime that negatively affects productivity?
  6.5.4. Do our systems easily track Key Performance Indicators?

### 6.6. Human Resources
  6.6.1. Are all departments performing at a high level?
  6.6.2. Do we need to hire more people to meet projected demand?
  6.6.3. Is our employee attrition level within industry standards?
  6.6.4. Do we need to improve our hiring process?

### 6.7. Finance
  6.7.1. Do we have strong financial controls in place? (AR, AP, payroll)
  6.7.2. Do we need to improve finance/accounting processes?
  6.7.3. Do we have access to working capital to support our growth plans?

Answering the current state questions should give you insight into what your Critical Success Factors (CSFs) should be. With this insight, select the three to five most important CSFs to achieve next quarter's goals. If a CSF is not listed below, you can add it to the list.

## Marketing Critical Success Factors
- Improve Niche Focus/Competitive Advantage
- Improve Brand/Messaging
- Increase Market Awareness – Execution
- Increase Advertising ROI/Improve Lead Generation
- New Product Launch

## Sales Critical Success Factors
- Improve Sales Conversion
- Improve Sales Process
- Increase Average Sale
- Improve Sales Channels

- Improve Sales Collateral
- Increase Pipeline (Booked Opportunities) – Execution
- Increase Pipeline (Open Opportunities) – Execution
- Define/Communicate Expectations for Customers

**Customer Service Critical Success Factors**

- Improve Customer Experience/Customer Care Process
- Decrease Customer Response Time
- Decrease Customer Handle Time (Improve Process)
- Up-sell Customers

**Operations / Delivery Critical Success Factors**

- Decrease Errors/Improve Quality
- Improve Efficiency (Gross Profit)
- Improve Fulfillment/Delivery Process

**Technology Critical Success Factors**

- Implement Systems to Improve Process and/or Efficiency
- Decrease System Downtime

**Human Resources Critical Success Factors**

- Increase New Hires to Meet Demand
- Improve People Utilization/Productivity
- Address Attrition Challenges

**Finance Critical Success Factors**

- Access Working Capital to Support Growth
- Find & Invest Capital to Support New Initiatives
- Improve Finance/Accounting Processes

## Leadership Assessment & Development Template

The Leadership Effectiveness Evaluation Template will help leaders understand what they are doing well and what can be improved. While many different leadership styles can be effective, there are three common principles consistently found in strong leaders:

1. Strong leaders earn the will of their team versus demanding respect — The key to long-term sustainability and employee motivation.

2. Strong leaders communicate clearly and wisely — Direction and expectations are fully understood by team members.

3. Strong leaders hold team members accountable for results — There are consequences for inaction or lack of effort.

The Leadership Evaluation begins with a 360-Degree Assessment. This assessment includes an introspective analysis as well as candid conversations with supervisors, peers and direct reports. After completing the assessment, the key findings are reviewed and action plans are created to leverage strengths and address leadership development opportunities.

## Introspective Leadership Analysis — Self-Assessment — The 7 C's of Success

A clear CONCEPTION of what we want, a vivid vision, a goal clearly imagined.

- Have I created my personal vision statement?
- What are our company's common vision and mission? Are they shared by all? Do they support my personal vision?

A strong CONFIDENCE that we can attain the goal.

- Am I confident I have the ability to meet or exceed my workplace expectations?

- What skills, knowledge and/or experience will help me improve my confidence level? (Professional Development Plan)


A focused CONCENTRATION on what it takes to reach the goal.

- Do I clearly understand our Critical Success Factors? Have I prioritized what is most important? Do I focus on the top priorities?

- Am I effective at time management? Do I spend time on activities that bring the most value to the company and myself?

- How much time do I spend on non-core/low-value activities? How can I eliminate, make more efficient or delegate?


A stubborn CONSISTENCY in pursuing our vision.

- Do my actions match my words? Do I walk the talk?


An emotional COMMITMENT to the importance of what we are doing.

- Am I committed to attaining both the company's vision and my personal vision?

- Am I emotionally committed to the company's values?

- Does my work role provide the workplace satisfaction I desire?

- Do I recognize others for their contributions? Do I make others feel important by showing genuine interest?

A good CHARACTER to guide us and keep us on a proper course.

- Do I make the right decisions at work and off work?
- Do I display integrity day in and day out?
- Do I act in a way that people will respect?
- Do I control my emotions? Do I manage disappointment effectively?

A CAPACITY TO ENJOY the process along the way.

- Do I look at each day as a gift?
- Do I take time to enjoy the journey?
- Do I have a good work/life balance?

## Supervisor Evaluation (People the Leader Reports To) – For 360-Degree Reviews

|  | Name | Name |
|---|---|---|
| Do I understand their preferred communication style? What is it? Reference Behavioral Style Chart in the People Management Chapter. | | |
| Do I adapt my communication behavioral style when appropriate? | | |
| Has the leader clearly communicated the company vision and mission with me? Do we share a common vision and mission? | | |
| Has the leader clearly communicated what is expected from me (i.e., roles, responsibilities, performance metrics, goals, etc.)? Am I meeting/exceeding these expectations? | | |
| What is working well? Why? | | |
| What is not working well? Why? | | |
| What can I improve upon? | | |
| How can my leader improve? Is the leader open to candid feedback? If not, how can we improve trust? | | |

**Peer Evaluation** (People the Leader Reports To) – For 360-Degree Reviews

|  | Name | Name |
|---|---|---|
| Do I understand their preferred communication style? What is it? Reference Behavioral Style Chart in the People Management Chapter. | | |
| Do I adapt my communication behavioral style when appropriate? How can my peers better adapt their style? | | |
| Do my peers share a common company vision and mission? | | |
| Do we clearly communicate expectations? Do we understand our roles and responsibilities? Am I meeting/exceeding these expectations? Are they? | | |
| What is working well? Why? | | |
| What is not working well? Why? | | |
| What can I improve upon? | | |
| How can my peers improve? Are my peers open to candid feedback? If not, how can we improve trust? | | |

**Direct Report Evaluation** (People the Leader Reports To) – For 360 Degree Reviews

|  | Name | Name |
|---|---|---|
| Do I understand their preferred communication style? What is it? Reference Behavioral Style Chart in the People Management Chapter. | | |
| Do I adapt my communication behavioral style when appropriate? How can my direct reports better adapt their style? | | |
| Does my team share a common company vision and mission? | | |
| Do I clearly communicate expectations? Does my team understand their roles and responsibilities? Are they meeting/exceeding these expectations? If not, why? | | |
| What is working well? Why? | | |
| What is not working well? Why? | | |
| What can I improve upon? | | |
| How can my team improve? Are my employees open to candid feedback? If not, how can we improve trust? | | |

## Leadership Effectiveness – Professional Development Plan

1. Define my Personal Vision
    a. Action plans to address the 7 C's of Success

2. Create Professional Development Plan
    a. Action plans to improve my leadership capabilities (skills, knowledge and relationships)

3. Action plans to improve my relationship/performance with my:
    a. Supervisors/Leaders

    b. Peers

    c. Direct Reports

## Leadership Effectiveness – Communication Tips from TTI, Ltd

If communicating to a **Persuader**, key points to remember:

Strengths -- Persuaders tend to:
- Get results through others.
- Be optimistic about goals.
- Utilize their intuition.
- Be decisive and aggressive when dealing with challenges.
- Initiate action plans through others.

Weaknesses-- Persuaders may:
- Not be good at time management.
- Not deliver on time.
- Overextend themselves.
- Lack follow-through.


If communicating to a **Promoter**, key points to remember:

Strengths -- Promoters tend to:
- Use social and verbal skills within the team.
- Bring unity to the team.
- Promote the ideas and people throughout the organization.
- Calm conflicts within the team.

Weaknesses-- Promoters may:
- Lack attention to details and be disorganized.
- Talk more than listen.
- Be overly optimistic about goals.
- Emphasize fun over profit.
- Act before thinking through a situation.

If communicating to a **Relater**, key points to remember:

Strengths -- Relaters tend to:
- Help others using empathy and understanding.
- Value both people and things.
- Listen well.
- Help people feel significant.
- Support others in achieving their goals.

Weaknesses-- Relaters may:
- Be too kind.
- Have a tough time being candid.
- Lack a sense of urgency.
- Not perform well under stress.
- Hold grudges.


If communicating to a **Supporter**, key points to remember:

Strengths -- Supporters tend to:
- Have patience and comfort others.
- Excel in a team environment.
- Like an environment where tenure matters.
- Want to follow established procedures.

Weaknesses-- Supporters may:
- Avoid change and prefer status quo.
- Hold grudges.
- Hesitate to move forward with new ideas.
- Avoid delegating tasks.

If communicating to a **Coordinator**, key points to remember:

Strengths -- Coordinators tend to:
- Work for a leader and a cause.
- Maintain high standards of conduct and work.
- Be quality-oriented and process-driven.
- Make decisions based on rules rather than emotions.

Weaknesses-- Coordinators may:
- Tend to avoid showing their true feelings.
- Resist change.
- Lack confidence in self and team.
- Become difficult to work with under stress.
- Overuse organizational procedures and not rely on intuition.


If communicating to a **Analyzer**, key points to remember:

Strengths -- Analyzers tend to:
- Maintain high standards and focus on accuracy.
- Focus on process.
- Use facts and data to solve problems.

Weaknesses-- Analyzers may:
- Lean on team leader or supervisor to make decisions.
- Hesitate to act without sufficient facts or precedent.
- Lack new ideas or don't think outside of the box.
- Not verbalize their feelings.
- Avoid delegating tasks.

If communicating to a **Implementer**, key points to remember:

Strengths -- Implementers tend to:
- Have creative ideas and think outside of the box.
- Start slow and finish fast.
- Challenge the team to achieve high performance.
- Manage time well.
- Calculate the ROI before making a decision

Weaknesses-- Implementers may:
- Become demanding under stress and insensitive to people's feelings.
- Under-appreciate others.
- Take on too much.
- Come across as insincere.


If communicating to a **Conductor**, key points to remember:

Strengths -- Conductors tend to:
- Be competitive and focus on winning.
- Enjoy solving problems and challenging assignments.
- Be results oriented.
- Be positive and optimistic.
- Like confrontation and debate.

Weaknesses-- Conductors may:
- Overstep authority within the team.
- Use fear as a motivator.
- Overextend their ego.
- Be poor or selective listeners.
- Lack tact and diplomacy.

# Niche Strategy/Competitive Advantage Template

This coaching template is often used in half-day strategy sessions to help company leaders develop their annual and quarterly strategic plans. In some cases it will validate the current strategy and in other cases it will help you innovate. Innovation can include process improvement, product development and/or expansion into new markets, services or products.

1. Core Strengths — Areas to Explore
    1.1. Industries where we have knowledge and connections.
    1.2. Customer segments within particular industries where we have knowledge and connections.
    1.3. Competencies / Expertise (i.e., specific solutions or processes where we have knowledge and connections. For example, a specific type of manufacturing, technology, distribution channel or service offering).
    1.4. Geographies — Knowledge or presence that can be leveraged and help differentiate our company (i.e., our team located in Charlotte, N.C.).
    1.5. Company offerings — How do we deliver better value than the competition? What is our price competitiveness?
    1.6. Company structure — What fixed assets can we leverage? Does our flexibility enable quicker innovation / product development?
    1.7. What are we passionate about?
    1.8. What strengths would we like to increase or add to our company? What resources are required to develop these strengths? Do we have the time and/or capital to develop the strengths?

2. Target Market
    2.1. What industries do we serve? What industries can we serve?
    2.2. What segments exist within each industry? (i.e., company size, location, types of products / services...)
    2.3. Evaluate trends and growth within each industry segment.
    2.4. Explore common challenges within each industry segment.

2.5. What other products or services will be valuable to our current customers? What challenges are our customers seeing that are not adequately being addressed in the market place?

3. Niche Strategy

    3.1. Which industry segment challenges can our strengths provide the most value? (i.e., What problems can we solve in the industry?)

    3.2. Among these industry segment challenges, where is the greatest ROI? What resources are required compared to potential profit?

4. Competitive Analysis

    4.1. What competitors target the industry segments identified in our niche strategy?

    4.2. What are their key sales / marketing messages?

    4.3. Evaluate competitors' strengths compared to our strengths (product/service value, delivery model, distribution model, price, guarantees).

    4.4. Identify our competitive advantage.

5. Marketing Strategy

    5.1. What messages will resonate best among prospects in our target market?

    5.2. Who are the key stakeholders, decision makers, key influencers within the industry segment and prospective companies?

    5.3. Where do decision makers and prospects look for information?

    5.4. What events do decision makers/key influencers attend? What associations do they belong to?

**Process Excellence**

Creating your Company Playbook provides a foundation for continuous improvement, creates scalability and ensures quality. Your Playbook documents your core processes and serves as a training platform for new employees. It decreases the ramp up time for new employees and decreases risk of "knowledge loss" (knowledge is not lost when an employee leaves the company).

Step One:  Identify your Core Processes for each business function

Your accountability chart should reflect your key business functions. During a leadership meeting, your functional leads should be able to quickly identify the core processes. Usually this takes less than an hour. For each of the core processes you should have a Process Owner (the employee responsible for performing the process or managing it).

Step Two:  Ask the Process Owner to document the high-level tasks in each Core Process

Delegating this responsibility does three things. One, it minimizes the time required by company leadership. Two, it increases employee ownership of the process. Three, it provides feedback regarding how well the employee understands the process.

You can use the Process Documentation template located in the process chapter.

## Step Three: Compile your documented processes to create your Company Playbook

After your core processes have been documented, you will have completed the last element of your company playbook — a living document that will change as your business evolves. Your playbook should be used as part of your employee onboarding process.

With your company playbook in hand you will increase both operational efficiency and your company value. I've observed this first-hand by coaching a business owner through an exit strategy. The acquiring company found tremendous value from the company playbook as it decreased the dependency on the existing business owner.

## Continuous Improvement

Process excellence begins first by eliminating unnecessary, low-value-add tasks and ends with designing the most efficient process flow. During your weekly leadership team meetings, you will tackle issues that involve your core processes. To address these issues it is helpful to refer to your Company Playbook and ask yourself the following questions:

1. Is the process being followed? If not, why? Do we need to address an employee's skill or knowledge? Do we need to improve the systems (i.e., software applications) supporting the process?

2. If the process is being followed and we are still encountering challenges, how can we improve the process?

3. If the process is improved, update the company playbook and provide the necessary training to all team members involved in the process.

## PROCESS TEMPLATE

| STEP | TASK | RESPONSIBLE ROLE | TOOLS USED | TIME FRAME |
|---|---|---|---|---|
|  |  |  |  |  |
|  |  |  |  |  |
|  |  |  |  |  |
|  |  |  |  |  |

## 90-Day Planning Agenda

Quarterly planning sessions ensure your leadership team is on the same page and provides a collaborative forum to prioritize company initiatives. 90-day planning sessions also provide the foundation for effective weekly leadership team meetings.

Depending on your company's complexity the first 90-day planning session can range from a half day to two days. Your second, third and fourth quarter planning sessions typically range from a half day to a full day.

Some companies prefer to start in January, but the timing cycle has little to no impact on your company performance. The mere exercise of planning and holding team members accountable is what drives business performance.

Companies we work with have found it very beneficial to bring in a strategic planning professional to facilitate the quarterly sessions. A third party facilitator should help you keep the meeting on track, avoid tangents, cut through company politics, and balance the conversation by preventing strong personalities from overwhelming the discussion.

We use the agenda below to facilitate the quarterly planning sessions. I've also included facilitator notes as part of the agenda.

1. Best Thing (Facilitator Note: Ask participants to describe the best thing that has happened over the last quarter — one personal and one business. This is always a good opener and helps set the agenda for a positive meeting)

2. Review the company's vision and mission. (Facilitator Note: The main purpose is to reinforce the vision and mission. After reviewing, ask the team, "Is this still relevant? If not, how should it change? If so, are we on track?")

3. Review the prior period's performance and KPIs. (Facilitator Note: Key Performance Indicators are important metrics that gauge the company's performance. This requires the company leadership team to do prep work for the meeting. As a facilitator you should probe the reasons for either meeting or exceeding the goals or reasons for not meeting the goals. Doing so will help you identify the critical success factors for the next quarter.)

4. Discuss the next quarter's goals. (Facilitator Note: The reason for the discussion is to make sure ALL Leadership team members believe the goals are reasonable and attainable. The goals should not be a slam dunk and should be within reach; otherwise the goals are meaningless.)

5. Define Critical Success Factors to achieve the goals. (Facilitator Note: For each goal, ask the team questions that probe the niche strategy, unique value, people, process and key partnerships that support the supply chain.) Questions include:

    5.1. Have we differentiated our product/service enough to provide a compelling value proposition to our customers?

    5.2. Do we need to improve a product or service? Do we need to add a new line? Do we need to discontinue an unprofitable line?

    5.3. Do we have the right marketing plans to generate enough prospects?

    5.4. Do we have the right sales process and the right sales people to close the opportunities?

    5.5. Can our operations deliver (people and process)? Are we ready to meet/exceed the customers' expectations (in quality, turnaround time, et cetera)? Is our process solid with the right applications in place for support?

    5.6. Is our customer service team ready to handle the projected inquires/problem tickets?

5.7. Do we have the right financial controls in place (AR, AP, working capital requirements)?

5.8. Do we have the right partners in place to support our supply chain? Have we communicated expectations and requirements?

6. Create Strategies and Action Plans for each goal. (Facilitator Note: Ask the leadership team to list both company initiatives that are currently ongoing as well as new company initiatives required to meet the quarterly plan. Once all of these initiatives have been listed, prioritize the importance.) Action Plan categories may include:

    6.1. **Must Have** — Quarterly performance will probably not meet or exceed goals without implementing

    6.2. **Strategic** -- Important, but not absolutely necessary to achieve next quarter's goals

    6.3. **Necessary** -- Company initiatives that are necessary for the company to operate, but add little value

    6.4. **Other** -- Company initiatives in this category should be questioned

7. Create Accountability. (Facilitator Note: Each company initiative should have one owner with a projected time to complete. Your list of initiatives will become a key part of your weekly leadership team meetings.)

8. Most Valuable Take Away. (Facilitator Note: At the end of the meeting ask participants what their most valuable takeaway is. This reinforces key messages discussed during the planning session.)

90-Day Plan Summary - Template

# Organization Name:
## 90-Day Plan as of <Insert Date>

### Mission

Why do customers purchase our products / services? (Incorporate your Unique Value Proposition & Niche Strategy)

Why should investors invest in us?

Why should employees want to work for us?

### 3 Year Vision

Annualized Revenue:
Annualized Profit:
# of Employees to Achieve Vision:
Products / Services Delivered:
Target Market (Customer Types, Geography, Niche Focus):

### Goals

| | Annual | Month 1 | Month 2 | Month 3 |
|---|---|---|---|---|
| | | | (90 – Day Goals) | |
| Sales | | | | |
| GP | | | | |
| NP | | | | |
| KPI #1 | | | | |
| KPI #2 | | | | |
| KPI #3 | | | | |

KPIs (Description)
KPI #1:
KPI #2:
KPI #3:

© 2012 Cornerstone Advisory Partners, Inc.

90-Day Critical Success Factors & Action Plans – Template

# Organization Name:
## 90-Day Plan Critical Success Factors & Action Plans

**CSF # 1:** _____

1.
2.
3.
4.
5.

**CSF # 2:** _____

1.
2.
3.
4.
5.

**CSF # 3:** _____

1.
2.
3.
4.
5.

List company initiatives / action plans to achieve each CSF. Identify person responsible and timeline for each initiative / action plan

© 2012 Cornerstone Advisory Partners, Inc.

## Weekly Leadership Team Meeting Agenda

1. Best Thing (one Personal; one Business)

2. Company News (Customers, Employees, Partners, Industry/Regulation Changes)

3. Company Scorecard — Last week's performance

4. Action Plans (Review progress on Company Initiatives created during 90-day Planning Session as well as new Action Plans created during Weekly Meetings)

5. Issues (Challenges within departments or an update on issues handled that may impact others)

6. Recap Action Plans created based on issues discussed

<u>Leadership Facilitation Guidelines:</u>

- Meeting times must be consistent and required.

- Meetings should be 90 minutes or less. Avoid going over 90 minutes unless an extremely urgent issue must be worked through. Eventually the meetings may take only 30 to 45 minutes unless critical issues require in-depth conversation.

- Avoid tangents — You will have to stop conversations from time to time.

- Control dominant speakers and solicit feedback from those who tend not to speak up.

- Avoid going through action plan detail that is not relevant to all.

- As issues arise throughout the week put them on the agenda to discuss during the weekly leadership meeting — Avoid the cycle of fire drills every day.

- Keep track of action plan status (open, closed) throughout the year – it provides a good summary of accomplishments.

## Coaching Engagement Project Plan

The Coaching Engagement Project Plan includes eight steps to implement the Performance Culture System in your company. The scope of the coaching engagement will vary based on your needs, availability and business complexity.

Our firm begins the engagement with a half-day planning session with the owner(s). After completing this meeting, we typically have enough information to layout the scope for the remaining seven steps. The project plan below will give you an idea of what this will look like.

1. Define the Vision (1/2 Day)

    1.1. Scope: Personal Vision, Company Vision, Company Mission, High Level Assessment, and Future Coaching Plan (Owner(s)' Perspective)

    1.2. Areas to Probe:

        1.2.1. Vision and Mission Shared by All?

        1.2.2. Assess Owner's Leadership Effectiveness

        1.2.3. Identify Key Leadership Team Members — Employees that should be involved in the Performance Culture Engagement

        1.2.4. Explore Current Challenges/Critical Success Factors: Competitive Advantage, Partners, Employees, Process, Leadership Effectiveness, and Finance (working capital and accounting controls)

2. Assess Leadership Effectiveness (Beyond the Owner)

    2.1. The 360 Degree Assessment —360 degree employee reviews provide candid feedback and help the Implementer build trust and rapport within the organization. The reviews also create alignment within the leadership team and allow the implementer to explain how Performance Culture will impact them personally (a key success factor in change management).

2.2. Workshop Facilitation (Included as part of 1/2 day planning session)

    2.2.1. What is working well (i.e., where employees are meeting/exceeding expectations)

    2.2.2. What's not working so well

    2.2.3. Evaluate trust inside the organization and leadership communication styles (DISC Assessment)

    2.2.4. Have leaders earned the will of their team?

    2.2.5. Evaluate employee accountability

    2.2.6. Evaluate consequences for inaction/poor performance

3. Leadership Planning Session Part 1 — Company Foundation (two 1/2 days or one full day)

    3.1. Performance Culture Overview

    3.2. Company Vision and Mission Shared by All

    3.3. Leadership Effectiveness (if 360 Degree Assessment is not done)

    3.4. Current State Assessment

    3.5. Accountability Chart (Today and Tomorrow)

    3.6. 2 x 2 Employee Expectations (Homework for next meeting)

    3.7. Company Value Chain — Foundation to define core processes (Homework for next meeting)

    3.8. What is our Competitive Advantage (If not clear, we can add a 1/2 day session to explore)

4. Leadership Planning Session Part 2 (1/2 day to full day)

    4.1. Employee / Team 2 x 2 Performance Ratings

        4.1.1. Evaluate why some employees are stars and why some are underperforming (knowledge, experience, training, coaching, process?)

        4.1.2. Action plans to leverage Stars and improve performance

    4.2. Review Core Processes

        4.2.1. What should we improve?

5. Deliverable — Company Playbook

    5.1. Mission and Vision

    5.2. Unique Value Proposition/Niche Strategy/Competitive Advantage

    5.3. Accountability Chart (Today and Tomorrow)

    5.4. 2 x 2 Employee Expectations

    5.5. Company Value Chain

    5.6. Core Processes Documented

6. 90 Day Planning Session (1/2 day to full day)

    6.1. Annual, Quarterly and Monthly Goals

    6.2. Critical Success Factors

    6.3. Strategies and Action Plans for the next 90 days

7. Weekly Leadership Team Meeting (two 90 minute meetings facilitated and two observed)

# ABOUT THE AUTHOR

Dallas Romanowski is the founder of both Performance Culture, Inc. and Cornerstone Business Advisors. Performance Culture is a performance management software and training company while Cornerstone is an executive coaching firm located in Wilmington, N.C. Dallas' talents include strategic planning, business coaching, advisory board facilitation, organizational management and finance. Dallas manages the IMAF Cape Fear Angel Fund and has invested in multiple entrepreneurial ventures.

Before founding Cornerstone, Dallas Romanowski was a business development executive for IBM, a management consultant for Accenture and a Department of Army Intern.

Dallas created the Performance Culture System to help his clients drive higher profits, develop great workplaces and support business succession plans. Performance Culture maximizes leadership effectiveness, increases employee productivity and morale, drives process excellence and develops winning strategies.

Outside of work Dallas enjoys spending time with his wife, Tessa and three children, Ben, Zak and Eva.